D1553968

Contents

DOI: 10.1057/9781137365699.0001

Preface

This book argues that it is crucial to talk to young people about gender as a primary step in violence prevention. It does this on the basis of empirical research with young people which strongly indicates the primacy of gender norms and expectations in shaping young people's views on what constitutes violence and what is seen as 'problematic' violence. Further, the data suggest that gender norms expressed in relation to violence are deeply entrenched and internalised by young people, and that in some cases, they do not explicitly acknowledge or recognise the ways they invoke gender to explain, justify or excuse violence. The findings point to the need to create physical and discursive spaces in which young people can achieve critical distance from these gender expectations, in order to challenge the norms which encourage an acceptance of particular forms of violence. There is increasing attention given to the potential of schools for challenging gender norms (Reay, 2006) and more specifically, for contributing to youth violence prevention. Policy-makers, child protection professionals and researchers have pointed to the transformatory capacity of schools in challenging hegemonic gender norms and behaviours. Recent debate has focused on the potential of personal, social and health education (PSHE), citizenship education and sex and relationships education (SRE) in particular, as curricular spaces in which gender-based violence might also be addressed. Data from the present project suggest that if schools are to address youth violence effectively, the focus of current provision must be expanded beyond child safeguarding, risk and criminality to include fundamental issues of gender and equality.

DOI: 10.1057/9781137365699.0002

Acknowledgements

I would like to thank the Society for Educational Studies for funding the regional study of young people and violence on which this book is based (Small Grant award, 2009). My deepest thanks go to the young people whose voices are represented in this book. The candidness and honesty with which they talked about their observations, experiences and understandings of violence allowed me to gain an insight into young people's conceptualisations of violence and violence prevention. I would also like to acknowledge and thank Dr. Claire Maxwell and Professor Nicole Westmarland for their invaluable comments on individual chapters of this book. Sincerest thanks also go to Dr. Melanie McCarry for reviewing the entire manuscript and for enriching its content and quality by doing so. I am deeply grateful for being able to draw on their collective expertise and insight.

List of Abbreviations

ASC	Annual Schools Census
BERA	British Educational Research Association
BME	Black or Minority Ethnic
CDC	Centre for Disease Prevention and Control (USA)
DCLG	Department for Communities and Local Government
DfE	Department for Education
DSCF	Department for Schools, Children and Families
EVAW	End Violence Against Women Coalition
FSM	Free School Meals
IDACI	Income Deprivation Affecting Children Index
IPV	Intimate Partner Violence
NASP	National Association of School Psychologists (USA)
NASUWT	National Association of Schoolmaster Union of Women Teachers
NSPCC	National Society for the Prevention of Cruelty towards Children
OCC	Office of the Children's Commissioner
PSHE	Personal, Social and Health Education
SRE	Sex and Relationships Education
VAW	Violence Against Women
VAWG	Violence Against Women and Girls
YPV	Young People and Violence

DOI: 10.1057/9781137365699.0004

Introduction

Abstract: *This chapter contextualises the focus of the project. It offers a brief overview of the impetus for the* Young People and Violence *study, as well as outlining key concepts and terms that are central to the book. It ascertains the need to involve schools in the endeavour to prevent violence among young people.*

Sundaram, Vanita. *Preventing Youth Violence: Rethinking the Role of Gender in Schools*. Basingstoke: Palgrave Macmillan, 2014. DOI: 10.1057/9781137365699.0005.

Why violence prevention, and why now?

How might we enhance violence prevention work aimed at children and young people? This book attempts to answer this question by drawing on empirical work with young people in the UK. The book seeks to extend current debates about the nature of violence prevention work and the role of schools in this endeavour. The research originated from a concern that traditional violence prevention campaigns were struggling to engage young people and to have an impact on their thinking and behaviour in relation to violence. In 2010, the UK government launched the *This Is Abuse* campaign, which intended to raise awareness about intimate partner violence among young people, and was re-launched in 2012 to accompany a revised national Action Plan to combat Violence Against Women and Girls (VAWG) (Home Office, 2013). The discourses circulating on discussion boards for the campaign website suggested that young people were resistant to key messages about the gender-specific pattern and dynamic of relationship violence, and the subtle and multiple forms which partner violence might take. Around the same time, several cases of domestic violence among young celebrity couples became public, with the case of singers Rihanna and Chris Brown receiving considerable media attention. Public debates about the violence inflicted on Rihanna, the subsequent arrest of Chris Brown and musings about whether or not Rihanna would 'forgive' him revealed that domestic violence might still be viewed as 'provoked' and that victim-blaming was widespread (Boston Public Health Commission, 2009; Hoover, 2014).

What can we do to challenge and change young people's views on violence? Historically, violence against/among young people has been conceptualised as a public health problem and more recently, in the UK, as a child protection or safeguarding issue. Violence prevention campaigns have therefore traditionally focused on child health and welfare, targeting risk factors such as alcohol and substance abuse, and more recently, 'troubled families' (Department for Communities and Local Government, 2013). The treatment-oriented (and increasingly, punitive) approach to violence prevention has been identified as problematic by a number of authors who have analysed the intimate link between violence and gender (Dobash and Dobash, 1992; Hamner and Saunders, 1984; Hearn, 1996; 2012; Kelly, 1988). Feminist scholarship has drawn our attention to the important role of gender in shaping young people's use and acceptance of violence (Barter et al., 2009;

DOI: 10.1057/9781137365699.0005

,i 886 29 752 Defective
please return

,9, 01-b

McCarry, 2009; 2010). Yet, whilst more recent violence prevention campaigns have expanded beyond the public health/child protection focus to emphasise gendered patterns of violence perpetration and victimisation, the significance of gender norms continues to be underplayed. This book contributes to and expands on this evidence base by illustrating the formative role of gender in young people's ideas about what constitutes violence and thus, their attitudes towards violence and violence prevention. This book therefore provides persuasive evidence that violence prevention aimed at young people must seek to challenge gender norms and expectations as a primary element.

Conceptual framework and key concepts

One of the key problems facing violence prevention might be one of definition; how do we define violence and how do we decide what type of violence is a priority to prevent among young people? Strategies tend to have been fractured, focusing at times on violent crime, at others on gang or group violence, and more recently, on domestic or partner violence. Each of these forms of violence has been addressed with a different approach and focus; boys are primarily targeted in relation to violent crime and gang violence (Home Office, 2011) and girls are predominantly addressed in strategies focusing on sexual exploitation and abuse (DCSF, 2009), which may be disconnected from other violence prevention initiatives. Violent crime is approached from a judicial perspective, while relationship violence is more frequently addressed through the lens of rights, respect and, increasingly, gender equality. This book departs from much previous work on youth violence in its view that various differs of interpersonal violence are underpinned by a common thread – hegemonic gender norms. The book seeks to uncover the ways in which gender features in young people's understandings of violence across multiple forms. It therefore argues that violence prevention aimed at young people should always adopt a gender lens, in seeking to illuminate the influence of gender norms of thinking and behaviour in relation to violence, and to educate young people about alternative expressions of gender identity which might challenge, resist and reject violence. While the book prioritises young people's own conceptualisations of violence, it is necessary to define the way in which violence is discussed and considered in this book.

DOI: 10.1057/9781137365699.0005

Defining violence

Violence has become increasingly recognised as a widespread social problem. It manifests itself in multiple forms, including violent crime, public disorder, child maltreatment, intimate partner violence and elder abuse, and within these categories, violence can be enacted physically, sexually, verbally, emotionally and financially (WHO, 2002; Bellis et al., 2012). Violence by and against children and young people has more recently received extensive attention in the media, by practitioners, researchers and policy-makers (Barter et al., 2009; Tutty et al., 2005; Wood et al., 2011). The National Society for the Prevention of Cruelty towards Children (NSPCC) estimates that 1 million secondary school pupils will have suffered abuse at some point in their lives (NSPCC, 2011) and the Crime Survey for England and Wales shows that young people aged 16 to 24 years are more likely to suffer violence than other adult age groups (Chaplin et al., 2011). Bullying and violent crime against younger children (aged 10 to 15 years) is also prevalent (Bellis et al., 2012), with nearly half of young people in a recent study reporting that they had been bullied at school (Chamberlain et al., 2010).

'Youth violence' will primarily be discussed in relation to interpersonal violence between individuals within this book, and specifically, intimate partner violence and so-called public violence (occurring between individuals not in an intimate relationship). It is defined as 'the actual or threatened use of physical, verbal or emotional power, intimidation, or harassment by or against individuals or groups, which results in physical and/or psychological harm, or is harmful to the social well-being of an individual or group of individuals' (Tutty et al., 2005, p.8). The other various forms of violences that young people may experience are fully recognised, including (but not limited to) state violence, war, trafficking and sexual exploitation and witnessing domestic violence between adults. In the *Young People and Violence (YPV)* study, the central focus was to explore how young people themselves understand the concept of interpersonal violence. The materials used in the focus groups depicted scenarios of emotional, physical and sexual violence between two individuals. In some scenes, both individuals were obviously teenagers (e.g. the scenario was set in a school); in others, both individuals were clearly adults (e.g. reference was made to adults within a marriage relationship) and in a few, this was more ambiguous. Vignettes and statements portrayed scenes about intimate relationships, whereas photographs

DOI: 10.1057/9781137365699.0005

portrayed a combination of intimate and non-intimate relationships. These materials were used as prompts for more general discussions about violence among young people.

Defining youth

This book adopts an explicit youth-centred perspective drawing on work in critical youth studies (Allen, 2011; Best, 2007; Fraser et al., 2004; Kehily, 2007). Central to the design of the project on which the book is based was a concern to do research with, rather than on, young people and to use a methodology that gave voice to young people, rather than to adults speaking on behalf of young people. The book positions young people as actively making meaning of their lived experiences, and views it as essential to understand the meanings young people construct around violence in order to effectively educate them about it. A concern to understand violence from the perspectives of young people is central, within the context of many existing initiatives that are dominated by adult views on what young people need.

The population of 'young people' spans a large age range, of course, covering children and adolescents in compulsory schooling, and young adults in further and higher education. Studies on young people and violence have focused on ranging populations, spanning pre-teenagers to young adults (Burton et al., 1998; Barter et al., 2009; McCarry, 2010; Chaplin et al., 2011). In relation to violence prevention, the youth population is typically defined as young people aged between 10 and 29 years (e.g. CDC, 2014; WHO, 2002; Pearce & Pitts, 2011), where the lower limit remains fairly consistent at age ten but the upper limit ranges from 21 to 19 years. Recent UK work on young people and interpersonal violence (e.g. Barter et al., 2009; McCarry, 2010) has focused on youth aged 13 to 18 years. As Barter et al. (2009) point out, terminology around youth and violence has often been slippery and vague, with terms such as 'young people', 'adolescents', 'teenagers' and 'youth' being used interchangeably to refer to young people aged under 18 years. In the present project, the focus was on young people in compulsory schooling and specifically on adolescents aged 14 to 15 years. This particular age group was selected on the basis of their cognitive competence to discuss a relatively complex, and potentially sensitive, issue (O'Kane, 2008), as well as the relevance of school-based initiatives to teach about youth violence to this age group. We know that violence in adolescent relationships is prevalent before the

DOI: 10.1057/9781137365699.0005

age of 16 (NSPCC, 2011) and it is therefore vital that we access young teenagers' understandings of violence. In this book, the terms 'youth', 'young people' and, on occasion, 'teenagers' will be used to refer to children aged 13 to 18 years and, when in specific reference to the YPV study, to young people aged 14 to 15 years.

Theoretical frame

The book draws on a number of theoretical frameworks, including critical masculinities, critical youth studies and feminist post-structuralism. The concept of discourse is central to the analysis presented in this book, particularly in its focus on the ways in which discourses around violence give legitimacy to particular ways of thinking and being (e.g. Allen, 2011; Sauntson, 2012; Weedon, 1987). The ways in which young people's talk, or discourses, about violence reproduce (and sometimes resist) gendered power inequalities is central to understanding the ways in which people's social identities are formed, but also to identifying potential sites for emancipatory social change and practice (Fraser & Bartky, 1992, p.178). Numerous authors have pointed to the relevance of this methodological framework for analysing the place of gender in talk and its significance with regard to what it can tell us about internalised and normalised enactments of gender (Cameron, 2001; Lazar, 2005; Wodak, 2008). Important work has been done to explore the ways in which people construct themselves (and others) in their spoken stories about violence (Anderson and Umberson, 2001; Cobbina et al., 2010; Hollander, 2001; Myrttinen, 2004). Gender difference is reflected and constituted through language used to describe a range of violences (e.g. Enloe, 2007). Particular discourses can be used to construct men and their violences as dangerous and 'serious', while women and women's behaviours (including violence) are seen as 'trivial' and about 'silly' matters (Anderson and Umberson, 2001; Hollander, 2001). Subjectivity and particular gender and sexual identities may be constructed through stories about violence, relationships and lived experiences and it is important to consider the ways in which young people, too, may construct particular versions of gender through their discursive rejection or acceptance of violence.

The definitions set out above have informed the search and review of existing literature in the field in order to delimit and distinguish studies that focused on collective violence, self-directed violence from those on interpersonal violence, and those studies that reported gender as a

DOI: 10.1057/9781137365699.0005

personal characteristic, but did not analyse it as a culturally and socially constructed set of expectations that might influence young people's thinking and behaviour in relation to violence.

Violence and schools

A key aim of this book is to explore ways in which the views of young people can inform violence prevention in schools. The potential of schools for addressing complex and sometimes challenging issues with young people, such as traumatic historical events, religion, death and sex and relationships has been long been debated by practitioners, policy makers and academics. These discussions have flourished in the context of considerations about the purpose of schooling (e.g. Davies, 2012; Epstein et al., 2012). Increasingly, attention has turned to the role and potential of schools in addressing and contributing to youth violence prevention. National policies such as the now-obsolete *Every Child Matters* (DfE, 2004) and the recent *Working Together to Safeguard Children* (DfE, 2013a) emphasise the right of children and young people to be safe and healthy, and the task of schools in helping young people to achieve this. It is steadily being recognised that early education and intervention, and multi-agency working, are key factors for influencing young people's attitudes in relation to violence. Schools are well-placed to promote non-violence (Varnava, 2009) and the duty on schools to protect children from bullying and violence on the basis of gender, sexuality and other protected characteristics is clear (Equality Act, 2010). There is therefore a critical need to expand our knowledge about the key issues schools should address in preventing violence among young people.

The *Young People* and *Violence* study

The YPV study was conceived from a desire to better understand how violence prevention work in schools might engage young people and influence their attitudes and behaviours in relation to violence. The study was designed to gain a clearer understanding of how young people conceptualise and make sense of violence and sought to answer four specific research questions:

DOI: 10.1057/9781137365699.0005

1   How do young people characterise violence?
2   What are the factors that influence young people's views on what
    constitutes violence?
3   Are some forms of violence viewed as more or less acceptable and/
    or inevitable than others?
4   What are the reasons underlying the perceived acceptability of
    some forms of violence relative to others?

This book is premised on the belief that violence prevention must
fundamentally address young people's conceptualisations of violence.
Our knowledge about how young people define violence is necessary to
being able to destabilise entrenched assumptions about what constitutes
violence, why it occurs, and how it might be prevented. However, we
currently know relatively little about how violence prevention might
better engage this population. The *YPV* study sought to contribute to this
knowledge by gaining an insight into young people's views on violence
and the assumptions that underlie their perceptions.

There is a clear and pressing need to address violence in same-sex
intimate relationships (McCarry et al., 2008; Donovan and Hester, 2008)
on an equal footing with relationship violence among heterosexual teenagers. The specific and, arguably, restricted focus of the *YPV* project was
chosen due to the exploratory nature of the research, and pragmatic and
ethical barriers regarding access to schools and participants. Given that a
primary objective was to explore how young people view different forms
of violence, it would have enriched the data had scenarios of same-sex
violence been included. Future research in this area should – and will –
address this gap.

Preventing youth violence: rethinking the role of gender in schools

This book contributes to existing knowledge about young people's
views on violence and extends this to consider the more specific factors
that need to be considered in violence prevention work and the role
of schools in delivering this. The book suggests, drawing on the voices
of young people in the UK, that gender underpins young people's
understandings of what constitutes violence, as well as when violence
is seen as problematic, acceptable, deserved or preventable. The study
revealed that their views on normative gender behaviour are central to
their conceptualisations of some forms of violence as unproblematic and

others as 'unacceptable', and their views on the preventability of violence. Young people's narratives revealed that gender norms were not always explicitly recognised by participants, and that their discourses around violence often exposed deeply entrenched and internalised expectations of gender. The role of schools in preventing violence focused primarily on punitive discourses and young people in a number of schools expressed a desire for schools to punish violence more harshly than they currently did. Only a handful of young people discussed pro-active and positive preventative measures that schools might take in seeking to influence young people's attitudes at an early stage. None of these involved challenging gender stereotypes that might encourage violence. This book will argue that in seeking to tackle youth violence, schools must address gender norms and expectations among young people as a primary element. In order to impact young people's thinking about violence schools should seek to challenge and destabilise young people's views on normative gender behaviour. This necessitates schools' moving away from a child protection or safeguarding focus in relation to violence and to rethinking the role of gender in their work to prevent youth violence.

This book makes the case for placing gender centrally and initially in violence prevention work in schools in the following way: Chapter 1 briefly reviews existing work on youth violence, paying particular attention to the focus of previous research and prevention campaigns. It highlights the need to include youth voice in developing violence prevention. Chapter 2 re-examines the link between gender and violence, reminding us of the fundamental influence of gender on use and views of violence. Further, given the emphasis on youth as active makers of meaning in their own lives, the chapter suggests that we should pay attention to how young people assert their expectations of gender through discourses about violence. Chapter 3 outlines the design and methodology of the *YPV* study, with a particular focus on the youth-centred approach. Chapter 4 presents the findings of the study with regard to young people's characterisations of violence. It discusses the factors influencing what young people perceive to be violence and whether it is seen as problematic or not. Chapter 5 analyses the production of gender norms in young people's discourses about violence. It suggests that not only do young people's views on violence reflect internalised gender behaviours, but that they actively make claims about their expectations for gender behaviour in their stories about violence. Their narratives about violence as un/deserved, un/acceptable and un/preventable produce particular

DOI: 10.1057/9781137365699.0005

meanings about gender. Chapter 6 discusses the role of schools in preventing youth violence, as a precursor to exploring youth perspectives on school-based violence prevention in Chapter 7. Young people's views on violence prevention suggest that schools might take a more consistent zero-tolerance approach to violence. Further, given the centrality of gender to young people's understandings of violence, schools should re-think the fundamental role of gender in their violence prevention work.

DOI: 10.1057/9781137365699.0005

1
The Case for Youth-Informed Violence Prevention

Abstract: *This chapter offers an argument for thinking about youth violence prevention from the perspectives of young people themselves. It suggests that young people's understandings of violence must be sought and used in developing targeted violence prevention initiatives. The chapter reviews existing literature to illustrate the prevalence of violence among young people, as a basis from which to consider the necessity of targeted prevention work.*

Sundaram, Vanita. *Preventing Youth Violence: Rethinking the Role of Gender in Schools.* Basingstoke: Palgrave Macmillan, 2014. DOI: 10.1057/9781137365699.0006.

Introduction

This chapter contextualises the focus of the book in several ways. Firstly, it provides an argument for thinking about youth violence prevention from the perspective of young people themselves. The chapter reminds us that violence among young people is widespread and that violence prevention aimed specifically at youth should be a priority. In presenting the case for focusing on youth perspectives on violence prevention, the chapter will first provide a brief overview of research on youth violence. The specific emphasis will be on interpersonal violence within and outside of intimate relationships. Then, an argument will be made for using youth voice in violence prevention work, drawing on international and national child rights frameworks. The chapter will then go on to explore the predominant models for youth violence prevention, arguing that these may be restricted in their reach and potential for engaging youth.

Young people and violence

There is a pressing need to re-focus our attention onto violence among young people. Violence has historically been used by young people as individuals and in groups to assert social power or dominance in relation to others. This includes school bullying, intimate partner violence and gang violence. Violence among young people constitutes an enduring social concern in many societies (World Health Organisation, 2002; 2010), and existing research indicates that violence among young people is widespread. A significant portion of the literature about youth violence has focused on dating violence by young men towards women and girls, and has explored risk factors associated with perpetration and victimisation (Ackard et al., 2012; Barter et al., 2009; Burton et al., 1998; Ely, 2004; Foshee et al., 2013; Martin del Campo et al., 2012; Howard et al., 2013; McCarry, 2010; Noonan and Charles, 2009; Palmetto et al., 2013; Stader, 2011; Temple et al., 2013; Vagi et al., 2013; Wekerle and Tanaka, 2010). There also exists a wide body of evidence on violence among young men (DeKeseredy and Schwartz, 2005; Messerschmidt, 2005; Mills, 2001; Newburn and Stanko, 1995; Wilson and Daly, 1985) and much of the literature has focused on specific populations or has foregrounded particular characteristics of the sample. For example, studies

DOI: 10.1057/9781137365699.0006

have been done on violence among working-class men, alcohol or drug abusers, young offenders or homeless young men (Gorman-Smith et al., 2004; Maschi and Bradley, 2008; Vitacco et al., 2010; Willis, 1977). The theoretical literature which seeks to analyse why young men engage in violence has concentrated more specifically on the role of gender in producing, encouraging and sustaining violent behaviour (Connell and Messerschmidt, 2005; Hamlall and Morrell, 2012; Hearn, 2007, 2012; Messerschmidt, 2000; Mullaney, 2007; Totten, 2003). Increasingly, studies have been conducted to investigate the prevalence of violence by, and between, young women (Foshee et al., 2010; Herman and Silverstein, 2012; Martin del Campo et al., 2012; Osler, 2006; Osler and Vincent, 2003). Attitudes which are supportive of violence may already be well-established in adolescence and primary prevention among children and young people has been shown to succeed (Flood, 2007). Violence prevention aimed specifically at young people should therefore be a priority for governments, professionals working with young people and researchers alike.

Recognising youth voice in violence prevention

There have been calls for the views of young people to be more widely sought out and represented in violence prevention work aimed specifically at youth. Article 19 of the United Nations Convention on the Rights of the Child (UNCRC) (1989) gives children and young people the right to be protected from violence and calls on governments to ensure that children and young people are not neglected, mistreated or subjected to abuse. The UNCRC notes that children and young people should be informed about and participate in achieving their rights – including their right to be protected from violence. Further it states that children who are capable of forming their own views should be given the right to express those views freely in matters affecting them (Article 12). The Office of the Children's Commissioner (OCC) for the UK is guided by the UNCRC in its pledge to seek out, take seriously, and act upon the views of young people in relation to issues which concern them. The mission of the OCC similarly states that the perspectives of young people should shape decisions that are made about their lives, and that research should therefore involve young people and children to ensure that their voices are heard (OCC, 2013).

The British Educational Research Association (BERA) has called for more educational research to be conducted on young people's experiences

DOI: 10.1057/9781137365699.0006

of violence and their views on violence, in order for child-led violence prevention initiatives to be developed (Brown & Winterton, 2010). The strength of consultation with young people to inform policy and practice has been noted in numerous recent studies (Fielding and Bragg, 2003; Flutter, 2006; Rose & Shevlin, 2004). Young people themselves state that it is important that they be encouraged to express their own opinions on sensitive and contentious issues, rather than simply being told how to behave and that their actions are 'wrong' (Burton et al., 1998). The latter point may be particularly relevant in relation to violence prevention, which has typically employed a directive approach to instruct young people on 'what not to do'.

Youth voice in existing violence prevention work

An increasing number of youth violence prevention campaigns have been developed at the national, regional, local authority, and school level in the UK. The vast majority have been based on an adult-led understanding of violence and mechanisms for preventing (and typically for responding to) violence. Typical models for violence prevention tend to teach young people 'what violence is' and seek to dissuade them from engaging with it (Banos Smith, 2011). School-based programmes focus on discipline and control to prevent perpetration, teaching about risk reduction strategies to avoid victimisation, mechanisms for disclosing abuse, and resources and skills to support victims (Greytak, 2003).

Young people's own understandings of violence are rarely acknowledged and used as the basis for school-based violence prevention work with youth. Prevention campaigns frequently use official definitions of violence as a starting point (Home Office, 2010; Welsh Assembly Government, 2010) and adopt a prescriptive stance in terms of dictating behaviour to young people (Banos Smith, 2011) (exceptions to these will be discussed in Chapter 2). This may lead to time-limited gain in terms of attitudinal changes, resistance from young people to messages being promoted, and a restricted understanding of young people's views on violence and factors underlying their involvement in or acceptance of violence (Barter et al., 2009; Fredland et al., 2005; Hester and Westmarland, 2005; McCarry, 2003, 2007, 2009, 2010; Stanley et al., 2011). Research which seeks to uncover and *change* young people's attitudes towards violence has commonly tended to use predetermined characterisations of violence for participants to comment on or respond to (Burton et al.,

DOI: 10.1057/9781137365699.0006

1998; Fox et al., 2013b; Simonson and Subich, 1999; Smith et al., 2005; Sommer et al., 2013; Ulloa et al., 2008; Yick, 2000). These studies have undoubtedly made a significant contribution to our knowledge about young people's relationships to violence. However, the use of pre-defined descriptions of violence may lead to a partial understanding of (factors shaping) their views, as well as an incomplete picture of their experiences of violence. It is argued here that violence prevention campaigns which do not incorporate youth perspectives on violence may struggle to engage young people at best, may lead to negative changes in attitudes and behaviours at worst, and may not reduce violence among young people. The following chapter will discuss existing violence prevention campaigns in the UK, focussing specifically on issues which might be important to engage young people with.

DOI: 10.1057/9781137365699.0006

2
Re-Establishing the Link between Gender and Violence

Abstract: *This chapter argues that youth violence prevention must fundamentally acknowledge the link between gender and violence. The chapter re-visits the well-established link between gender and violence with reference to seminal and recent research in the field. This research is used to remind the reader that gender can be seen not only as reflected in and through acts of violence, but as preceding and producing violence. A more specific understanding of the ways in which gender influences young people's views on violence is crucial to developing violence prevention.*

Sundaram, Vanita. *Preventing Youth Violence: Rethinking the Role of Gender in Schools.* Basingstoke: Palgrave Macmillan, 2014. DOI: 10.1057/9781137365699.0007.

DOI: 10.1057/9781137365699.0007

Introduction

This chapter aims to establish a focus on gender-based violence, by re-asserting the link between gender and violence with reference to seminal and recent research in the field. This chapter argues that in terms of violence prevention, the link between gender and violence should be re-examined and expanded. The analysis will suggest that gender education must be the primary component of anti-violence education. The treatment of gender as one of many (equally) contributing factors to violence maintains a reactive, rather than preventative approach to violence prevention. The link should be expanded such that we consider not only how gender might produce violence, but how it organises young people's views on what actually constitutes violence, why violence might be used, when it should not be used, and views on violence prevention. It is vital that we understand the ways in which gender mediates and structures these beliefs about violence in order to challenge the underlying norms which influence attitudes towards violence. It is argued that focusing solely on changing attitudes towards violence through punitive or disciplinarian approaches will be unlikely to be effective. We need to acknowledge and understand how young people relate to, give meaning to and interpret violence in order to be able to challenge and destabilise these perceptions.

Re-asserting the link between gender and violence

The World Health Organisation (2002) has recognised that violence exists in multiple forms (as discussed in the Introduction). Violence can be defined as collective, self-directed or interpersonal and can occur in multiple, overlapping forms across the lifecourse. The particular focus of this book is on interpersonal violence. Interpersonal violence itself encompasses multiple types of violences, which may be co-occurring or used interchangeably within the same contexts or relationships (Kelly, 1988). This includes physical, emotional, verbal, sexual, financial violence or cyber-abuse. Analyses of interpersonal violence reveal that men are primary perpetrators of violence (Chaplin, 2011; Office for National Statistics, 2012; 2013) and that this is the case across all forms of violence. A number of competing explanations for this gender bias have been advanced, including those which draw on biology, poverty

DOI: 10.1057/9781137365699.0007

and socialisation (Gurian, 2002; Watson, 2007). The theorisation of men's use of interpersonal violence has been greatly extended and enriched by feminist scholarship. A wide body of feminist scholarship has established a link between men's violences and gender expectations, norms, stereotypes and roles (Burton et al., 1998; Connell, 2001, 2002, 2005; Flood, 2001, 2010; Hearn, 1994, 1996, 1998, 2004, 2007; Kimmel et al., 2005; McCarry, 2007, 2009, 2010; Morgan, 1987; Stoudt, 2006; Totten, 2003). Violence has been argued to reflect and sustain particular versions of masculinity, through material acts of violence, as well as discursive and visual representations of violence (Hearn, 1998). Stanko (2002, p.33) has argued that popular images of violence rest upon unquestioned assumptions about and understandings of gender and of masculinity, in particular. The link between masculinity and violence thus becomes naturalised to such an extent that men's use of violence may be viewed as inevitable, normal or even justifiable (by virtue of their very nature). Indeed, one way in which violence may become legitimated is through a process of normalisation which is so effective that the violence itself 'disappears' (Morgan, 1987, pp.180–183). With no intention to diminish the fact that many women live in perpetual fear of violence from men as an 'ordinary' aspect of their daily lives (Dobash and Dobash, 1992; Hamner and Saunders, 1984; Kelly, 1988; Stanko, 1990), it is noteworthy that less attention has been given to men's fear of violent crime despite their consistent position as the primary perpetrators and victims of serious interpersonal violence (Stanko, 2002). It might be argued that this absence in the literature serves to reinforce a construction of violence as a routine aspect of men's experiences, thus amplifying the link between masculinity and violence.

What is meant by gender?

While gender is conceived of as central to explaining men's use of violence, it cannot be defined singularly in relation to violence. Masculinity in itself is certainly not viewed as static and universally manifested in all male bodies; indeed, constructions of masculinity are sufficiently variable to warrant pluralising the term to masculinities (Connell, 2005; Hearn, 2007; Morgan, 1987). Hegemonic masculinity is a key concept in understanding the gender basis of violence. It has been well-theorised as culturally and socially dominant and/or valued enactments of masculinity (Connell, 2005). These understandings of masculinity include the valorisation of aggression, demonstrations of physical strength, and expressions of

DOI: 10.1057/9781137365699.0007

physical, sexual and social dominance (Kaufman 2001; Kenway and Fitzclarence, 1997). However, it is vital to note that the present study does not see understandings of masculinity (or, indeed, of violence) as uniform in different contexts. It must also be recognised that there are contradictions between what is socially and culturally valued and what individual men do. Men can thus 'adopt hegemonic masculinity when it is desirable; but the same men can distance themselves strategically from hegemonic masculinity at other moments' (Connell and Messerschmidt, 2005, p.841). Here, it is useful to draw on Hearn's (2004;2012) conceptualisation of the 'hegemony of men' which acknowledges the distinction between the power of men as a social category and the power of men as individual agents. Hearn notes that not all men are violent, of course, but that complicity in men's use of violence is widespread. Many men (and women) reject violence against women and girls, but may engage in other practices which subordinate women and create or contribute to contexts which are conductive to violence. This can span engagement with the sex industry, viewing domestic violence as a 'private matter' or justifying the use of partner violence. With regard to exploring teenagers' attitudes towards violence, it is accepted that the narratives of young people regarding gender and violence may not necessarily be reflected in their subjective practices. Nonetheless, it is important to understand how and when complicit cultures develop, the factors underlying these, and how discourse can reflect or even produce contexts that are conducive to violence.

It is known that understandings of natural, appropriate and expected gender behaviour shape young people's use of violence, their acceptance of violence, their attitudes towards violence (Barter et al., 2009; LaCasse and Mendelson, 2007; McCarry, 2010; Messerschmidt, 2012; Próspero, 2006a, 2006b; Sears et al., 2006) and, therefore, their engagement with violence prevention campaigns and non-violence education. It is argued here that in order to change attitudes towards violence and eventually to reduce and eliminate youth violence, the factors underlying these ideas must be openly addressed. Existing evidence strongly suggests that this should entail an explicit focus on gender as an antecedent to anti-violence work.

Existing UK violence prevention campaigns

There has been a renewed focus on violence prevention among young people, particularly on VAWG following the coalition government's

DOI: 10.1057/9781137365699.0007

launch of a dedicated Action Plan in 2013 (Home Office, 2013). Existing campaigns can be broadly divided into those that are concerned with general awareness-raising about violence, including avenues for prevention, support and disclosure, and those which aim to change attitudes particularly through education. In the UK context, youth violence has most frequently been conceptualised as a child protection or child safeguarding issue and the focus of teaching resources and awareness-raising is therefore on respect for oneself, self-esteem raising, being safe and techniques for rejecting violence. Recent governmental publications on the role of education in preventing teenage violence suggest that violence prevention among young people continues to be viewed primarily in terms of awareness-raising about personal safety and rights, rather than as a gender-based issue which requires teaching to promote attitudinal change (DCSF, 2010a, 2010b; DfE, 2012).

In past campaigns, the response to violence has historically been conceptualised in secondary or tertiary terms. The emphasis has thus been on responding to victims of violence, rehabilitating perpetrators of violence and preventing future violent events from occurring. It has been noted that primary prevention should take a longer-term approach to preventing violence, imagining a future without any violence by 'changing attitudes, values and structures' which produce and sustain violence (Hester and Westmarland, 2005, p.15). There exists a robust body of evidence which highlights the influence of conservative gender norms and expectations on attitudes towards violence (Barter et al., 2009; Burton et al., 1998; LaCasse and Mendelson, 2007; McCarry, 2010). Further, research suggests that young people in the UK hold fairly traditional attitudes about gender roles (Equal Opportunities Commission, 2001; Mandel and Shakeshaft, 2000; McCarry, 2010), suggesting that these views must be challenged in order to combat acceptance of violence. In other words, focusing predominantly on supporting victims, punishing perpetrators or creating deterrents for future violence will not alter the underlying values and social arrangements which produce and sustain violence.

Despite the robust evidence base which exists about the gender basis of interpersonal violence, many existing violence campaigns have not engaged seriously with gender as an underlying cause of violence. Primary prevention initiatives have featured gender as one 'risk factor' among others (for perpetrators and victims), including drug and alcohol abuse, depression, lack of self-esteem, reduction of weapon

DOI: 10.1057/9781137365699.0007

use, emotional impulsivity and lack of awareness about personal safety (www.actiononviolence.co.uk; Home Office, 2010, 2012; Welsh Assembly Government, 2010). Gender is invariably mentioned in violence prevention work as there is global evidence and acknowledgement that men are the primary perpetrators of violence – and in relation to relationship or intimate partner violence that women are the primary victims of violence. The governmental Action Plan on VAWG demonstrates gender-awareness in its unambiguous focus on multiple forms of gender-based violence. It emphasises the need for early intervention and opportunities to challenge attitudes and behaviours that underpin and condone violence against women and girls. The role of teachers in tackling violence-supportive attitudes is explicitly recognised and teaching about sexual consent and healthy relationships is advocated. These are welcome advances which assert the need to tackle underlying causes of violence, not only to respond to violent behaviour, and which plainly signal that schools have a role to play in this endeavour. However, the reasons underlying gender-based violence are addressed less clearly and consistently and especially so, in relation to the work of schools. Thus, while girls may be specifically targeted in terms of teaching about self-esteem, respect and rejecting violence, the salient and mediating role of gender in negotiating these three is not addressed. Further, there are few clear statements about gender identities, masculinity and violence and the need to destabilise these links.

The governmental *This Is Abuse* campaign (launched originally in 2010 and re-launched prior to the publication of the Home Office Action Plan on VAWG in 2013) seeks to raise awareness among young people about multiple forms of partner violence and sources of survivor support. It addresses violence by men towards women and focuses explicitly on this gendered dimension of intimate partner violence in campaign resources. Despite this, gender norms and expectations were/are not critically addressed on the campaign website[1] or in associated materials. Indeed, some resources and polls on the site are devoted to challenging the perception that only women are victims of violence. A section entitled 'Myths about abuse' notes that 'anyone', including boys, may be victims of relationship abuse. The campaign defines abuse as happening when a controlling, aggressive or dominating person is involved, but does not address the gendered basis of these power differentials. On the website, masculinity is addressed solely in the context of young men potentially experiencing shame around disclosure of abuse. Moreover, the

DOI: 10.1057/9781137365699.0007

discussion board on the *This Is Abuse* website in the months following the campaign launch revealed that a number of young people accessing the campaign site continue to be resistant to the notion that men are the primary perpetrators of violence, referring to the campaign as 'sexist'. It is therefore vital to understand how young people themselves view violence in order to be able to challenge problematic, inaccurate – and even violence-propagating – understandings. Simply dictating to young people that violence is wrong and presenting them with facts about violence may lead to resistance to and rejection of these messages.

Expanding the link between gender and violence

In order to take a genuinely preventative approach to violence, the absence of an explicit acknowledgement of gender as a cause of violence (not as simply associated with violence) in violence prevention campaigns may be viewed as problematic. This book argues that in terms of violence prevention aimed at young people, the link between gender and violence should be restated. Firstly, violence prevention work must include a clear acknowledgement of the role of gender stereotypes and expectations in producing violence. Gender norms should be viewed as central to men's violences towards each other, as well as towards women and girls. It is maintained that violence prevention cannot be effective without an explicit examination of why it is men who are the primary perpetrators of violence and how current, prevailing constructions of masculine behaviour normalise violence among men. It is undoubtedly complex to maintain a clear focus on gender and the gender of men specifically, without isolating young men and boys or being seen to label all men as potential abusers. However, the widespread complicity in men's violence (Hearn, 2012) should also be analysed as a product of particular gender relations which may coerce non-violent men (and women) to remain silent, accept, witness and thereby be complicit in relation to violence.

This book suggests that the relationship between gender and violence might be expanded to incorporate a fuller understanding of the ways in which gender norms and expectations not only produce (and are reflected in) violent behaviour, but how they organise young people's thoughts about violence and what might be done to prevent violence. Gender is thus seen as being constituted in material acts of violence but also at the discursive level, through young people's visualisations and

DOI: 10.1057/9781137365699.0007

representations of violence. Effective violence prevention would seek to make explicit the influences that organise young people's productions and experiences of the 'life world' (Holstein and Gubrium, 1998, p.138), and this includes gender. The unambiguous focus on gender as an antecedent to, and central component of, violence is doubly important because of the commonsense and taken-for-granted nature of gender expectations. They must be made visible for young people in order to give them the opportunity to critically reflect on them and to consider alternative ways to be, think, feel and act in their life worlds.

The World Health Organisation's (2002, p.ix) World Report on Violence and Health reminds us that the widespread nature of violence means that it is often seen as an inevitable part of the human condition – a fact of life to respond to, rather than to prevent. Education has a vital role to play in trying to *prevent* violence from occurring at all. Schools are spaces and places in which gender norms and expectations are asserted, produced, sustained and policed by teachers and by pupils alike (Francis, 2008; Greytak, 2003; Jackson, 2002; 2003; Reay, 2001; Renold, 2006; Skelton, 2006; Skelton et al., 2009). Therefore, schools are spaces which have the potential to introduce and encourage alternatives to binary and hegemonic gender identities. They have the potential to play a key role in disrupting the gender norms that underlie and produce violence, and are reflected through enactments of violence. There exists evidence to suggest that primary prevention aimed specifically at challenging school cultures and pupil attitudes can effectuate change with regard to views on violence (End Violence Against Women Coalition, 2011; Foshee et al., 2005). While there is less evidence about whether changed attitudes lead to a lasting reduction in violence (Anderson and Whiston, 2005; Hester and Westmarland, 2005; Whitaker et al., 2006), some research does suggest that anti-violence work in schools may at least teach young people about developing healthy relationships in the long-term (e.g. Foshee et al., 2005; Hester et al., 2000; Maxwell et al., 2010; Mullender, 2001; Wolfe et al., 2009).

Campaigns that have been designed in collaboration with women's rights organisations, charities or refuges which have an explicitly feminist ethos have produced resources and launched campaigns which plainly promote the need to challenge gender stereotypes and expectations. Recent campaigns by the Home Office (2013), The White Ribbon Campaign (2013), End Violence Against Women Coalition (2011), Womankind Worldwide (2010) and the Home Office in collaboration

DOI: 10.1057/9781137365699.0007

with Women's Aid (2010) address gender stereotyping and attitudes around masculinity and femininity as fundamental to include in teaching and learning resources about violence. Curriculum materials for teachers explicitly encourage critical reflection on expectations of masculinity in particular (Home Office, 2010), and suggest using 'compensatory pedagogy' to help young people develop behaviours that might be discouraged by gender stereotypes and norms (van de Veur et al., 2007).

Hester and Westmarland (2005) and Cerise (2011) have reported on a number of school-based campaigns against violence, which explicitly prioritise a focus on gender equality. They note that in primary and secondary school settings in the UK, emphasising gender education as a fundamental component of anti-violence work, results in young people critically reflecting on their own experiences, feelings and views about violence. The projects reviewed focused on gender stereotypes, sexist language, the objectification of women, consent, and the normalisation of violence within media and pornography (Cerise, 2011). One challenge that was identified in delivering a sustainable programme of prevention work was the attitudes of some teachers, who did not feel comfortable with a perceived 'confrontational' approach to addressing gender and violence (Hester and Westmarland, 2005). This finding suggests that anti-violence work should include whole-school gender education aimed at teachers, as well as pupils. Whilst the focus of the campaigns reviewed here was on domestic, or relationship, violence, a central question being asked in this book is whether gender features centrally in young people's perceptions of violence across its multiple forms, and if so, how this knowledge might be utilised in preventative initiatives. This re-analysis of the link between violence and gender also entails expanding the predominant focus on child protection and safeguarding within schools, to include a serious consideration of gender equality in relation to violence.

Note

1 www.thisisabuse.direct.gov.uk (Accessed 3 August 2013).

DOI: 10.1057/9781137365699.0007

3
Capturing Youth Perspectives on Violence: Approaches and Techniques

Abstract: *This chapter describes and discusses the methodology used for the* Young People and Violence *study. It pays particular attention to the ways in which young people's views were sought and discusses the specific – and unique – combination of instruments that were used in the study. The chapter explores the fundamental role of youth-centred methodology in seeking to gain a fuller understanding of young people's relationship to violence. The case for focusing on discourses about violence to understand young people's gender expectations and behaviours is made.*

Sundaram, Vanita. *Preventing Youth Violence: Rethinking the Role of Gender in Schools.* Basingstoke: Palgrave Macmillan, 2014. DOI: 10.1057/9781137365699.0008.

Introduction

This chapter will describe and discuss the methodology used in the *YPV* study, paying particular attention to the way in which young people's views on violence were conceptualised in this study, the specific combination of instruments used in the focus groups that were conducted and the focus on young people's talk about violence. The chapter highlights the ways in which the conceptual framework and methods used for this study enabled a distinctive investigation of young people's views on violence. It explores the fundamental role of youth-centred methodology in seeking to understand young people's perspectives on violence and in making a contribution to knowledge about effective violence prevention.

This chapter will begin by reviewing existing studies which have sought to understand young people's views on violence. It will then go on to argue that the majority of existing work has focused on young people's views on particular forms of violence, and in particular, on partner, dating or relationship violence. It will be suggested that a broader focus on youth perspectives on what constitutes violence is vital to understanding how myths about violence among young people, and their acceptance of and involvement in violence might be addressed. The specific methods used for the current study will be described in detail, acknowledging the existing research which has informed the construction of instruments here. The chapter will subsequently discuss the focus on narratives of young people (Denzin & Lincoln, 1998; Polkinghorne, 2007). This focus is fundamental to appreciating how expectations of gender shape young people's understandings of violence and how young people characterise, make sense of and explain violence. It is argued here that young people's story-telling about violence reveals and reaffirms salient expectations and norms for gender behaviour, which simultaneously define (or not) violence, explain violence and even justify violence. In conclusion the chapter will consider the implications of research resulting from this particular use of methods for practitioners, researchers and policymakers.

What has been done already?

Youth violence

Studies researching violence among youth have frequently utilised survey or questionnaire methods to estimate the prevalence of violence

DOI: 10.1057/9781137365699.0008

among a given population and associated risk factors or predictors for being exposed to, or perpetrating, violence. Standard measures include asking retrospectively about experiences of violence in the past three months, six months or year (Foshee et al., 2013; Helweg-Larsen et al., 2004; Mitra et al., 2013; Sundaram et al., 2008; Turner et al., 2013; Zweig, Dank et al., 2013), or the use of psychometric scales and constructs to assess involvement in particular risk-taking behaviours (Chapman et al., 2013; Lohman et al., 2013; Shortt et al., 2013; Walsh et al., 2008). Important work has also been done using qualitative methodology, such as focus groups and in-depth interviews and these have often explored experiences of violence among specific groups of youth, for example, teenage mothers, female perpetrators of violence or juvenile offenders (Ausbrooks, 2010; Barter et al., 2004; Barter and Renold, 2000; Bibou-Nakou et al., 2013; Haglund et al., 2012; Herman, 2013; Honkatukia et al., 2006; Pösö et al., 2008; Próspero, 2006; Sullivan et al., 2012; Sullivan et al., 2010; Wang et al., 2007). The majority of studies have focused on dating violence among adolescents, although notable exceptions exist (for example, Renold and Barter, 2003) and few studies have explicitly sought to elicit young people's own conceptualisations of violence (Honkatukia et al., 2006; McCarry, 2010; Próspero, 2006b; Renold and Barter, 2002). In most previous research about interpersonal violence and young people, different characterisations of interpersonal violence (e.g. gang violence, domestic violence, sexual exploitation) have been analysed as detached from one another. Studies have not usually explored young people's views across different forms of violence or investigated commonalities or contradictions in conceptualisations, for example, in views on perpetrators of domestic violence and gang violence. It is argued here that this theoretical separation between forms of relational violence may have led us to overlook or underplay the salience of certain factors in young people's understandings of violence across a range of forms. Gender has been identified as a central and common factor which influences young people's attitudes towards relationship violence. Knowledge about its role in shaping views on other forms of violence enables the development of targeted work to contest these gender norms in teaching about violence.

The methods used in the *YPV* study have enabled a contribution to the literature on young people and violence in two ways. Firstly, the present study was specifically and distinctly focused on young people's understandings of what constitutes violence. This substantive focus led

DOI: 10.1057/9781137365699.0008

to the development of methods which aimed to elicit young people's own definitions and characterisations of violence, rather than using pre-determined definitions for them to discuss and comment on. The instruments used here facilitated discussion – or story-telling – by young people, through which particular understandings of violence were revealed. The prioritisation of young people's own conceptualisations of violence has implications for the development of violence-prevention initiatives, as well as for future research on violence and young people.

Secondly, the present study adopted a more generalist focus in relation to violence, rather than focusing on one specific form of violence. It used a combination of instruments to prompt discussions about different types of violence, which included intimate partner violence and stranger violence. Textual and visual representations of violence portrayed scenarios with a male perpetrator and female victim, a male perpetrator and male victim, and a female perpetrator and male victim. It was hypothesised that young people would characterise male-on-male, male-on-female and female-on-male violences as distinct from one another and that some of these would be viewed as acceptable, while others would be viewed predominantly as unacceptable. It is argued that the relatively expansive lens used here has allowed for common factors underpinning young people's understandings of multiple forms of violence to come to the fore.

Gender, youth and violence

Previous studies of the gender–violence link have most frequently focused on intimate partner violence. Existing youth-focused research has primarily investigated the role of gender expectations in shaping views on dating violence and, less so, on group or gang violence. The latter has tended to be explored among specific populations, such as with young people in socio-economically deprived areas (for example, Li et al., 2002; Maimon and Browning, 2012; Taylor et al., 2008), while more national studies have investigated youth views on relationship violence (Barter et al., 2009; Burton et al., 1998). The present study therefore represents a departure from predominant approaches in its concern to explore young people's accounts of violence more generally and to understand the place of gender in shaping views on what 'counts' as violence or not.

DOI: 10.1057/9781137365699.0008

Young People and *Violence*: design and methods

Accessing schools and participants

This book presents research that was based in the north-east of England. A total of six secondary schools were sampled for the study and within each school a total of 10 to 12 pupils were randomly sampled for participation in focus groups. Sample schools were selected from the Annual Schools Census (ASC) database. The ASC collects information about individual pupils and information about the schools themselves, including school size, faith status and gender composition. The individual pupil information collected includes free school meal eligibility, ethnicity, special educational needs, attendance and exclusions (DfE, 2013b). Sample schools were purposively selected on the basis of their faith status, gender composition, ethnic mix and socio-economic mix (where eligibility for free school meals (FSM) was used as an indicator of pupil deprivation) (DCSF, 2009). Publically available Income Deprivation Affecting Children Index (IDACI) scores were used to indicate area-level deprivation and provide additional contextual information. The IDACI score for each pupil does not relate directly to their individual family circumstances, but is a proxy measure based on their local area.[1] Gender composition was determined by whether the school is a single-sex or co-educational institution. Ethnic diversity was described as high or low according to the percentage of pupils who are categorised as White British. Deprivation was described as high, medium or low on the basis of the percentage of pupils who are eligible for FSM in the school and the IDACI score for the area. Two replacement schools with matching characteristics were selected for each sample school. Of the six sample schools, four were single-sex and two were co-educational. The characteristics of the sample schools are shown in Table 1.

It was considered important to sample schools that would allow for potential variations in views to emerge across culture, ethnicity, religion, class and gender. As Yick (2000, p.30) has argued, cultural groups have their own overriding values, worldviews and perceptions, which will influence individuals' attitudes towards social and cultural phenomena. While the *YPV* study was small-scale in nature and was not intended to be representative of all young people in the UK, or even in the north-east of England, the selection of young people from a wide range of educational institutions bolstered the external validity of the findings

TABLE 1   *Characteristics of sample schools (faith, gender, socio-economic and ethnic mix)*

School name	Faith status	Gender composition	Deprivation status	Ethnic composition
Butterfield Grammar School	None	Single-sex boys	Low	88% White British
Saint Nicholas College (R)	Roman Catholic	Mixed-sex	Medium	81% White British
Saint John's School	Church of England	Mixed-sex	Low	66% White British
Sydney School for Girls	None	Single-sex girls	High	84% White British
Weeping Willow Boys School (R)	None	Single-sex boys	High	1% White British
Fishergate Girls School	None	Single-sex girls	Medium-High	1% White British

R = replacement school

generated by working with participants drawn from a spread of contexts (Glaser and Strauss, 1967).

Of the six sample schools, four agreed to participate after the first telephone contact. One school declined to participate, and in another school it was not possible to reach an appropriate member of staff to discuss the research with even after several attempts to telephone the school were made. For the latter two schools, pre-identified replacement schools were contacted using the same procedure as for sample schools. Both the replacement schools agreed to participate in the study following the first telephone contact to the school. It should be noted that one of the replacement schools (Weeping Willow Boys School) had a higher percentage of black or minority ethnic (BME) pupils (99%) than the original sample school (87%) and a higher percentage of pupils eligible for free school meals (31%) than the sample school (19%).

It was of primary importance to represent the perspectives of the young people in each of the schools. Their words are therefore used widely throughout to illustrate and evidence the analysis regarding their understandings of violence. In order to provide some context about the speaker, each quotation is preceded by the name of that pupil's school. Pseudonyms have been assigned to all pupils whose words are being cited in the book. In each school, participants were given the option to select their own pseudonyms but very few pupils chose to do so.

DOI: 10.1057/9781137365699.0008

In each school, the head of year or head of subject was asked to randomly select 10 to 12 students from their register to participate in two focus groups. In co-educational institutions, teachers were asked to compile separate lists of all girls and boys in their class and to randomly select an equal number from each of these lists. Each focus group comprised five to six participants and in mixed-sex settings, there were approximately equal numbers of girls and boys in each group. Two focus groups were held on the same day in each school. The focus groups were held in immediate succession so participants in the separate groups would not have had the opportunity to speak to each other about the topics discussed before they participated. There are no strict guidelines regarding the optimal number of focus groups to be held for a small-scale study and existing literature reviews suggest that there is considerable variation between studies (Bryman, 2008; Deacon et al., 1999). I was concerned to ensure that a range of voices were heard within each school and it was important to be able to ascertain the generalisability of views expressed within each setting. The latter, in particular, would not have been possible had a single focus group discussion been conducted in each school. It would have been difficult to know whether views expressed by pupils in this group were specific to those pupils or whether they were shared by others in their year group. It has been suggested that enough focus groups have been conducted at the point when patterns in the discussion data begin to repeat themselves and the researcher can anticipate what might be said in subsequent groups (Calder, 1977; Lunt and Livingstone, 1996). This was certainly the case in terms of the total number of focus groups conducted across schools in the present study, where themes emerged repeatedly across schools.

Focus group discussions

Focus group discussions revolved around a set of materials, which were identical for each focus group and for each school. These materials included vignettes or short written scenarios, statements and photographs, on which participants were asked to comment. The materials are described in detail in subsequent sections. It was of key importance that participants in the study were enabled to comment on this topic interactively, with reference and in response to the views of their peers, and that they could foreground the issues that they perceived to be of importance. Focus group discussion was selected as an appropriate method for the

DOI: 10.1057/9781137365699.0008

aims of this research, as it allowed for young people to jointly construct meanings about violence (Bryman, 2008; Denzin & Lincoln, 2005). The focus group format enabled participants to challenge each other's views, to reflect on and modify their own views after listening to their peers, and to introduce topics that they deemed to be of importance to understanding violence. Further, the discussions allowed me to identify group norms that were being established within and across groups.

The participants in this study were aged between 14 and 15 years and were enrolled on a full-time basis in Year 10 of school in all the settings that were visited. This particular age group was considered cognitively competent to reflect and comment on a relatively complex topic (James et al., 1998; Wood, 2003). It has been argued that focus group settings can encourage open conversation about otherwise embarrassing or difficult topics for young people (Kitzinger, 1994). Further, the interaction between participants presented opportunities for exploring their own definitions and understandings of violence, as well as to highlight similarities and differences in their beliefs (O'Kane, 2008). This was particularly useful in working with this age group, where views of peers may be influential in shaping, reaffirming or changing one's own position (Bryman, 2008). Semi-structured individual interviews might have been used to elicit youth perspectives on violence and might have allowed for young people to be more open and honest when removed from the gaze and viewpoints of their peers. Individual interviews could also have enabled more in-depth probing of young people's understandings of different forms of violence. However, given the emphasis on the construction of meaning in this study, and the lens adopted here that meaning is never constructed by individuals in isolation from other influences (Blumer, 1969), focus group discussions were considered more suitable. Focus group discussions revolved around the use of vignettes, statements and photographs. Each of these will be described in detail and reflections on their utility for generating interactive discussion between participants will be offered.

Vignettes

A vignette is a short story or scenario which provides 'concrete examples of people and their behaviours on which participants can comment. The researcher can facilitate a discussion around the opinions expressed.' (Hazel, 1995, p.2). The vignettes constructed for the present study told short stories about different forms of violence, hereunder verbal, physical

DOI: 10.1057/9781137365699.0008

and sexual violence or coercion. Participants in the study were asked to respond to the circumstances and characters presented in each of the vignettes and a series of standard prompts were used initially to facilitate discussion. A growing body of interdisciplinary work has used vignettes to explore a range of social issues among young people, including violence among adolescents (Barter and Renold, 2000), young people in care (Moules, 2009) and gender norms (Felmlee and Muraco, 2009). It is increasingly acknowledged that vignettes may be useful to examine normative perspectives on a given issue although it is difficult to establish how far participants' answers reflect the way they themselves would behave in the circumstances depicted in the vignettes (Bryman, 2008). Young people in this study were asked to discuss sensitive and potentially upsetting issues, including causes of violence, such as unhappy relationships, and experiences of violence, which included those in school, in the community and at home. The ethical implications of this are discussed further on in this chapter. Finch (1987) has argued that when focus group discussions deal with a sensitive topic, respondents may feel that they have to produce particular types of response. However, the fact that vignettes depicted imaginary scenarios about other people permitted a degree of distance to be established between respondents and the questions they were being asked to consider and might therefore have been perceived as less threatening.

Original vignettes were constructed for this study on the basis of opinions on violence that had been expressed by young people in existing research. Próspero's (2006b) work documented adolescents' perceptions of behaviour in dating relationships and appropriate behavioural responses. He found that young people of both genders anticipated aggressive behaviour in response to particular scenarios they were presented with. The behaviour presented in Próspero's scenarios was used as the basis for vignettes constructed for the present study. A second source of information for the vignettes was the *This Is Abuse* campaign. The campaign website contained multiple videos of different scenes of violence between young people in an effort to illustrate the myriad of ways in which violence might be manifested and the vast continuum of behaviours that should be considered as violent. As discussed in Chapter 2, when the campaign was launched in 2010, the discussion boards on the website revealed enormous resistance from guests to the page, who rejected the notion that violence was primarily perpetrated by boys against girls, and who dismissed the idea that 'lower

DOI: 10.1057/9781137365699.0008

level' forms of violence, such as slapping, should be considered violent. These opinions and the video scenarios presented on the website were used to develop stories for the vignettes in the present study. Each vignette was written with a male perpetrator and a female perpetrator in order to explore whether young people responded differently to the same scenario being acted out by a male or female perpetrator.

A sample vignette which was used in this study is presented here. This vignette intended to depict physical and verbal aggression.

> Steve is playing around with his girlfriend's phone and sees that she has received many texts from another boy in their year. When Steve asks his girlfriend about this, she says that she should be allowed to have male friends and he should stop getting upset about nothing. Steve pushes his girlfriend and calls her a 'slut'.

Each vignette was printed on an A3-sized card and participants were presented one vignette at a time. First, the story was read aloud to them by me, then the vignette was placed centrally on the table they were seated around to give them an opportunity to read the vignette. After each reading, I asked participants a series of prompts ('what do you think X is feeling?'; 'what do you think X is thinking?'; 'what do you think X should do?'). These prompts initiated an interactive discussion that started with reference to the specific vignette that had been read, but frequently expanded to include more general examples of violence or aggression that participants had encountered. The discussions allowed participants to express their views on what constituted violence, when violence was justified, who had the right to be violent, and to relate these key issues to their own experiences of violence. Vignettes were effective in terms of provoking discussion among participants and allowed for violence to be discussed primarily in a detached way, rather than in relation to the young people's own use of violence (although some boys did refer to their own and other people's use of violence against them or against family members). This element of distance may have facilitated young people to talk openly about their views on violence, as they were able to disassociate themselves from any use of violence while seeking to explain why 'other people' might be violent in different situations. One or more of the prompts was usually used to initiate discussion and the inclusion of characters, a storyline (which most participants identified as familiar) and settings which were recognisable to the participants formed the focus of lively discussion in the majority of schools. Patterns

DOI: 10.1057/9781137365699.0008

emerged in young people's understandings of violence, including what they thought constituted violent behaviour, explanations for the use of violence by characters in the vignette, judgements on whether violence in this scenario was acceptable and judgements on whether violence of this kind was acceptable in a more general sense.

Statements

The second type of instrument used in the study was short statements. Statements were one-sentence assertions about physical, sexual and emotional/verbal violence which participants were asked to agree or disagree with and to discuss in relation to their answer. Statements can be a useful tool for exploring young people's views as well as the process of coming to those particular views through interaction and discussion (O'Kane, 2008). Ranking exercises in particular necessitate discussion, prioritising and sorting of issues (O'Kane, 2008, p.140) and, in the present study, allowed an insight into the factors that influenced, mediated and shaped young people's identification of violent behaviours and explanations offered for these. In terms of discussing complex issues, statements represent a concrete position or scenario for younger participants to anchor their discussions, explanations and negotiations in.

Statements were developed on the basis of views expressed by young people about violence in previous research, for example, that violence towards a woman is acceptable if she has been unfaithful (Burton et al., 1998; Barter et al., 2009; Sears et al., 2006). Each statement was presented with a female and male perpetrator in order to explore whether young people's views on violence varied according to perpetrator gender. Statements drew on assertions about violence that had been expressed by young people in UK and North American research. The intention was thus that each statement would realistically reflect views held by young people across geographical settings and that they would stimulate discussion. An example of a statement about physical violence was 'It is acceptable for a man to hit a woman if he knows she has been cheating on him.' A sample statement about sexual violence was 'It is acceptable for a man to expect sex from a woman who has been flirting with him over a long period of time.' A sample statement about emotional violence was 'It is acceptable for a man to yell at his partner if she has done something to make him jealous.'

Statements were printed on card so they could be circulated among each focus group for participants to read individually. Each group was

DOI: 10.1057/9781137365699.0008

asked first to rank the statements with regard to how strongly they agreed with them. The ranking was done through group discussion and nego-tiation about each statement. Secondly, each statement was taken in turn and discussed with specific reference to the perpetrator of the violence in order to understand whether violence perpetrated by a woman against a man was perceived differently to violence perpetrated by a man against a woman, and the reasons underlying this if so. The closed nature of statements should not necessarily preclude interactive and spontaneous discussion (O'Kane, 2008). As Christensen & James (2008, p.159) have pointed out, whilst participatory activities (including ranking exer-cises) in themselves provide a source of data, the dialogue taking place around these activities provides an even richer insight into participants' interpretations, understandings and meanings. In the present study, the statements used primarily elicited direct responses (predominantly 'yes' or 'no') rather than stimulating narration. However, once probed to explain their responses more fully, participants did recount situations in which their friends or acquaintances had experienced violence and expand on when violence might be necessary, deserved, unacceptable or understandable.

Photographs

The third instrument that was used in the focus groups was photographs depicting threats and acts of violence. All depictions of violent threats or actions were of physical violence only. The use of photographs and other visual media in work with children and young people is increasingly being recognised as a way in which to engage this age group effectively (Christensen and James, 2008). It has been argued that visual images can stimulate young research participants' interest in and enthusiasm for a topic. Further, it offers a means by which to make sensitive, embarrassing or challenging topics more accessible by presenting tangible examples of what a particular issue 'looks like'. The notion that photographs – or indeed young people's reflections on photographs – is evidence of an objective reality has been contested (Allen, 2011). The focus here was less on what was actually occurring in each of the photographs or how accurately participants were able to articulate this, and more on how young people made sense of the images, interpreted what they saw and explained the interactions that were depicted. Whilst not intending to dismiss the material reality that the selected photographs depicted (e.g. two bodies in a particular form of interaction, set in a particular

DOI: 10.1057/9781137365699.0008

location), young people's narratives were prioritised as significant to understanding the processes by which they attributed meaning to the acts represented.

The photographs were sourced from the internet using search terms which included 'male on male violence', 'male violence against women', 'woman fighting man' and 'men fighting'. No photographs of female-to-female violence were sourced as a primary concern here was to explore how young people's views on men's violences might differ, for example, violence between men compared with men's violence against women. Photographs depicting military conflict or state violence were excluded as the focus of the study was interpersonal violence. Photographs which depicted severe and visible injuries and blood were excluded due to the young age of participants and institutional ethics committee requirements. It was the original aim to include photographs of women enacting violence towards men; however, extensive internet searches resulted in very few useable images. The vast majority of images were cartoons or scenarios staged obviously for comedy or theatrical effect. For this reason, no photographs of women perpetrating violence against men were included in the final selection. The photographs that were selected depicted threats of violence (e.g. one individual shouting, intimidating or physically threatening another) or acts of physical violence (e.g. slapping, punching or pushing) between two men or by a man towards a woman. While identical depictions of violence between two men and between a man and a woman could not be sourced, photographs of similar situations were selected.[2]

Each photograph was printed on an A3-size card so that it could be circulated among focus group participants prior to and during the discussion. A series of prompts ('what do you think of this photograph?', 'how does this photograph make you feel?', 'what do you think is happening in this photograph?') were used to initiate discussion and when young people mentioned violence (which they did in all of the groups), probes into why they thought a given scenario was violent were asked. In the YPV study, young people were presented with photographs that had already been taken by others, rather than photographs of violence that they had taken themselves. It has been argued that using young people's own images of a given topic enables their perspectives to come to the fore (Allen, 2009). However, due to the challenging nature of the topic and clear, related ethical considerations, it was not feasible to ask young participants in this study to take their own photographs depicting

DOI: 10.1057/9781137365699.0008

violence. Instead, the selected photographs were used to prompt focus group discussions about what constitutes violence. It has been argued that the use of photographs on their own may simply produce young people's comments about pictures (Christensen and James, 2008) and that these may not offer any insight into their interpretations of an issue. However, when triangulated with other methods photographs can encourage a concentrated focus on a given topic and can allow it to be explored from different perspectives. In this study, it became apparent that contradictions existed in young people's understandings of what constituted violent behaviour and their justifications for using violence depending on the medium through which violence was presented.

Photographic images of violence produced a different response to textual scenarios about violence. The inconsistencies emerged in the ensuing discussion about the photographs and stories, rather than with direct reference to the materials themselves, and they provided a unique insight into the different factors which might mediate young people's views on violence. The photographs provided an immediate and gripping stimulus for discussion. Participants often laughed or made jokes about the images initially and then moved on to relating the scenarios to their own experiences, narrating stories about violence they had witnessed, violence towards friends and, in some cases, violence that had been perpetrated towards themselves. In the vast majority of groups, all the photographs were named as depicting 'violence' but the discussions revealed that some of these instances were viewed as less serious or less violent than others.

Ethical considerations

A number of ethical considerations and procedures were followed in designing and implementing the *YPV* study. The topic of violence is sensitive, even when it does not involve directly asking people about their own experiences of violence. It is an issue which might potentially cause anxiety, fear or distress in terms of viewing and discussing materials which depict violence, as well as recalling own experiences of witnessing, using or being subjected to violence (Campbell and Dienemann, 2001; Fontes, 1997, 2004; King and Churchill, 2000). In the present study, participants were all young people aged under 18 years, and this reinforced the need to consider the impact that discussing violence might

DOI: 10.1057/9781137365699.0008

have on them. In designing the study, I adhered to the ethical guidelines set out by the BERA with regard to research with children and vulnerable young people (BERA, 2011). BERA guidelines specify the imperative to consult with young people on matters affecting them and to ensure that the research design allows them to express their views freely. This was considered carefully in relation to designing instruments for focus group discussion, as well as with regard to seeking fully informed consent from participants. Further, BERA guidelines state that when researching topics which might provoke distress, measures should be put in place to reduce this and to safeguard participants. This involved liaising with parents and schools before gaining access to young people, as well as making arrangements with each school to provide whole-class and individual support following the focus groups.

Prior to obtaining permission from sample schools to speak with their pupils, a covering letter explaining the aims and scope of the study and written consent forms were sent to parents of all Year 10 pupils in each school. Only pupils whose parents had given consent for their participation were entered into the sample from which focus group participants were selected. The vast majority (98%) of parents across all schools gave their consent for their child to participate in the study. Parental consent forms were sent directly to the named teacher at the school, who sent out one reminder to parents ahead of arranging the times for focus group discussions with me. Information sheets about the study and consent forms were sent to participants ahead of the focus group discussions. The information sheet detailed the aims of the study, the nature of the participants' involvement in the study, how and why their school had been selected, what their data would be used for and how it would be reported. The consent form reiterated the purpose of the study, what participants were being asked to do, reminded participants of the voluntary nature of their participation and of their right to withdraw from the study. All the pupils who had been selected for the focus groups read and signed a consent form and no pupils who had been selected declined to participate in the study.

Each school made arrangements to address issues relating to youth violence, relationship abuse and personal safety in a whole-class setting following the focus groups. These topics were addressed within a Citizenship Education or PSHE (Personal, Social and Health Education) lesson in most schools. Pupils who participated in the group discussions were given information about a named member of staff whom they could

DOI: 10.1057/9781137365699.0008

contact should they feel anxious or distressed following their participation in the study. While arrangements were made for pupils to seek
support should they feel disturbed by the issues discussed during the
focus groups, there were fewer guidelines available about actions to be
taken if violence was disclosed during focus group discussions. Several
young people disclosed that they had experienced violence from stran-
gers and on the street. A very small number of pupils disclosed experiences of abuse from partners (always narrated as being ex-partners) and
family members. All participants were guaranteed that their responses
would be treated confidentially in any reporting of the research. This
necessitated reflection on procedures to be followed if concerns about
child safeguarding were raised in the process of conducting focus groups.
It was decided that unless it became apparent that a young person was
in present, frequent and/or short-term danger, disclosures about violent
experiences would not be reported to a teacher. When experiences of
violence were talked about in the group discussions, care was taken to
spend the final five minutes of the discussion talking to participants
about victim support, resources they could draw on in the community
and in school, and the importance of reporting bullying and other forms
of violence to a trusted adult. I also reminded them of the arrangements
put in place with the school following the research.

Detailed ethical procedures were followed at the institutional (HEI)
level prior to implementing the study. An ethics audit form detailing the
purpose of the study, age of participants, methods and instruments to
be used, means of obtaining informed consent and feedback loops was
completed and submitted for review by the departmental ethics committee. The committee consists of academic, student and 'user' representa-
tives who reviewed a full project proposal alongside the ethics audit form.
More information was required regarding the number of adults who
would be present during the focus groups and the use of photographs
of violence. Once the necessary information had been provided and
approval had been granted by the ethics committee, contact was made
with sample schools.

Listening to young people's talk about violence

The primary focus of the study was to explore and gain an understanding of how young people make sense of violence, and the underlying

DOI: 10.1057/9781137365699.0008

factors which characterise this process. The concern with interpretive practice, the way in which 'the life world ... is produced and experienced by its members'(Holstein and Gubrium, 1998, p.138), necessitated a phenomenological lens to interpret and analyse young people's talk about violence. The unit of analysis was young people's narratives, stories and accounts of violence.

As Denzin and Lincoln (2005, p.641) remind us, 'we know the world though the stories that are told about it.' Narratives tell us how people make sense of the world, how they act in the world and how they expect others to act in the world (Chase, 2005; Franzosi, 1998). In terms of exploring how young people understand what constitutes violence and the factors which influence and shape these perceptions, an analysis of their talk about violence was revelatory. Orbuch (1997, p.455) has noted that narrative accounts 'represent ways in which people organise views of themselves, of others, and of their social worlds'. In the present study, narratives about violence exposed the deeply entrenched gender norms which shape young people's views of violent behaviour – and of the 'life world' around them. Cobbina et al. (2010) note that feminist scholarship has a long-standing tradition of analysing the ways in which gender is produced and reproduced through language and that this work has shown how the structure, content and use of language not only reflects, but constitutes, gender inequality (Cobbina et al., 2010; Cameron, 1998). It was a key aim to analyse the ways in which gender featured in young people's talk about violence. A distinctive feature of this analysis was an interest in the ways in which gender is produced and constituted through narratives about violence, as well as how gender expectations is reflected in these accounts.

Focusing on spoken accounts about violence thus revealed the ways in which young people situate themselves and others in relation to violence and the mediating role of gender norms and expectations in this regard. Qualitative analysis of oral narratives, 'thinking about narrative not simply as a form of text but as a mode of thought' (Bruner, 1997, p.64), thus allowed an exploration of how and *why* young people think about violence in ways which survey design or attitudinal research does not. It should be acknowledged that in my own analysis and presentation of young people's narratives I may be seen to be privileging an analytical agenda which my participants do not share (Chase, 2005, p.664; Denzin, 1997). By assuming an authoritative voice in interpreting their talk I could be accused of distancing myself from my narrators' own voices.

DOI: 10.1057/9781137365699.0008

However, as Chase (2005, p.664) argues, the aim of this particular form of analysis is to make visible 'taken-for-granted practices, processes and structural and cultural features of our everyday social worlds'. This necessitates a different – but not dismissive – voice to that of my speakers. There was a concern here to illuminate the ways in which young people use their 'stocks of knowledge' (Schutz, 1970) of socially originated ideas, values and attitudes to interpret their experiences, make them meaningful and interpret the actions, feelings and motivations of others (Holstein and Gubrium, 1998). It is, of course, relevant to note that the narratives presented and analysed in the book are not simplistic reproductions of young people's words, but must be considered in the context of the interactions between the participants and me. The discussions produced discourses, meanings and stories about violence and gender that were co-constructed and that were fluid and changing over the course of group discussions in some cases. That is to say, that I do not intend to present young people's narratives about violence as static or rigidly held viewpoints, but as versions of seeing and telling the world that might change over time, in different settings, with another group of peers or, indeed, another facilitator. The more interesting point was that the 'tellings of the world' in relation to violence and gender were consistent in many ways across focus groups, schools, girls and boys.

Template analysis was used to code and categorise the narrative data generated in focus group discussions across the six schools. This analytical style was selected on the basis that it allowed an iterative approach to analysing the narrative data, while maintaining a structure that was grounded in the existing literature about young people and violence (Miller and Crabtree, 1998). A coding template was devised that was loosely based on the research questions outlined in the study, as well as on categories of interest that had been defined in existing literature on violence and young people (Barter et al., 2009; McCarry, 2010; Próspero, 2006b; Burton et al., 1998). The template was revised and expanded as new and unanticipated themes emerged during data analysis. Recurrent theme analysis (Hernandez et al., 2012) was used to examine broader themes within and across participants' narrative accounts about violence. Links between the codes identified in the template and the emergent themes were explored to illustrate significant issues within participant narratives and across the sample (Hernandez et al., 2012). While I have sought to represent the voices of my participants as honestly as possible, by contextualising quotes with information about materials that were used to prompt the discussion and, where relevant, by including longer excerpts that situate the quotes within a fuller exchange, it has not always been feasible or desirable to provide large amounts of detail about the context of individual quotes. The use, positioning and interpretation of the quotes are ultimately chosen by me and the subjectivity inherent to this process must be acknowledged.

New insights

Using the combination of instruments and the analytical framework outlined here offers some new insights into young people's views on violence. The use of multiple materials to explore the same issue in this study allowed me to see how the presentation of violence could influence young people's perceptions of behaviours as more or less violent. The same forms and scenarios of violence were presented across the materials, but in one form the behaviour might be seen as unacceptable and very violent, whereas in another it might be seen as understandable and therefore as less negative.

The use of materials covering multiple forms of violence allowed an insight into the fundamental role of gender underlying young people's views of different forms of violence. The use of materials which were not introduced as being about violence *per se*, to elicit perspectives on what could be considered violent or not generated insights into the factors shaping young people's views. The focus on young people's narratives specifically came about after the data revealed the ways in which young people constructed stories about context, relationship dynamics, causes and patterns of violence to constitute some behaviours as violent and others as not, and some forms of violence as acceptable and others as not. As will be discussed in Chapters 4 and 5, these stories were heavily shaped by young people's expectations around normal and appropriate gender behaviour.

Notes

1 Deprivation status is accorded on the basis of percentage of pupils who are eligible for free school meals (FSM) and IDACI score. An IDACI score of 0.18 indicates that 18% of children aged under 16 in that Super Output Area are living in income-deprived families.

2 Photographs cannot be reproduced here due to copyright permissions.

DOI: 10.1057/9781137365699.0008

4
What Is Violence? Characterisations and Understandings of Violence

Abstract: *This chapter explores a central theme of the* Young People and Violence *study, namely, how young people understand violence. The chapter focuses distinctively on young people's own characterisations of violence, what they define as violent (or not) and the factors influencing their conceptualisations. The findings reveal that whilst young people name a range of behaviours as violent, they do not uniformly disapprove of, or reject, all of these. The chapter explores variations in young people's characterisations of violence as problematic or not, and analyses the mediating factors in these narratives. The findings point to the primary influence of gender norms and expectations in shaping what young people regard as (problematic) violence.*

Sundaram, Vanita. *Preventing Youth Violence: Rethinking the Role of Gender in Schools*. Basingstoke: Palgrave Macmillan, 2014. DOI: 10.1057/9781137365699.0009.

DOI: 10.1057/9781137365699.0009

Introduction

This chapter presents findings concerning young people's understandings of violence. Specifically, young people's views on what actually constitutes violence are addressed, taking into account factors which influence their definitions. Knowledge about young people's characterisations of violence is crucial to realising how and why young people come to accept and tolerate (and reject) different forms of violence. Further, understanding the circumstances which impact young people's views on violence is necessary to being able to target preventative efforts. The chapter first discusses young people's characterisations of what constitutes violence, reflecting on the range of views offered across the different materials that were used for the study. Secondly, young people's views on the primary perpetrators of violence are discussed, paying particular attention to the gendered assumptions that are made. Lastly, differences in young people's conceptualisations of 'what is violent' across varying victim–perpetrator dynamics are explored. Notions of 'understandable' and 'unacceptable', 'serious' and 'trivial' violence emerged depending on the assumed relationship and gender of the victim and perpetrator in the depictions offered.

What do we know already?

Some work has been done to understand how young people themselves define, categorise and characterise violence, but young people's experiences and understandings of violence have usually been measured according to pre-defined characterisations of physical, psychological or emotional, and sexual violence (Ackard et al., 2012; Foshee et al., 2005; Helweg-Larsen and Boving Larsen, 2006; Lohman et al., 2013). Further, violence prevention campaigns that have used these representations of violence have been met with resistance and hostility by young people (see for example, McCarry, 2003; 2009). Several, distinctive studies have sought to understand how young people relate to dating or domestic violence in particular (Barter et al., 2009; Burton et al., 1998; Feiring, Deblinger et al., 2002; Jackson et al., 2000; McCarry, 2009; 2010; Próspero, 2006b; Sears et al., 2006). These studies have found that violence among young people is pervasive (Burton et al., 1998; Barter et al., 2009). Further, adolescents express a high level of tolerance towards

DOI: 10.1057/9781137365699.0009

different forms of violence, defining various behaviours as 'typical' and even 'acceptable' depending on the context, the dynamic between victim and perpetrator and the gender of the victim and perpetrator (Dublin Women's Aid, 1999; Mullender et al., 2002; Próspero, 2006a; Sears et al., 2006). Young people define behaviours within relationships as violent in specific contexts and some forms of violence, for example, hitting or jealousy, are considered abusive only if they occur repeatedly or if severe physical violence is involved (Barter et al., 2009; Sears et al., 2006). Further, violent behaviours are also constituted as 'joking around' or even as caring in other contexts (Dublin Women's Aid, 1999; Sears et al., 2006, p.1197). There is evidence to suggest that definitions of abuse may also depend on the perceived intention underlying the behaviour (Mitchell et al., 2009). Sears et al. (2006) thus found that boys were more likely to employ motivation or intent as a criterion for defining behaviour as abusive, whereas girls characterised behaviour as violent if its impact was negative.

A number of authors have noted that violence perpetrated by young men (towards other men and women) is viewed differently to violence perpetrated by young women (towards other women and men). Violence used by girls is often trivialised and dismissed as 'silly', 'bitchy' and less serious, whereas the presumed physical power of boys is used to construct male violence as serious, threatening and more danger-ous (Cobbina et al., 2010; Hollander, 2001; McCarry, 2009; Sears et al., 2006; Wang, Petula and Ying, 2007). Accordingly, physical abuse is perceived as being carried out primarily by boys, whereas psychological or emotional abuse is perceived as being carried out by girls in the main (e.g. Cobbina et al., 2010; McCarry, 2009; Osler, 2006). A review of the literature suggests that young people's views on what constitutes violence is influenced by a myriad of factors and, further, is characterised by contradictions. Violence is sometimes defined by the intention behind the behaviour (Sears et al., 2006), while other studies find that multiple forms of abuse are viewed as a 'normal' (and unquestioned/able) aspect of an intimate relationship (Barter et al., 2009). Young people appear to associate domestic violence very strongly with male perpetrators (Ausbrooks, 2010; McCarry, 2009), yet they question the notion that men are the primary perpetrators of intimate partner violence (McCarry, 2003). Thus, gaps persist in our understanding of the issues that must be tackled in violence prevention aimed at youth. More knowledge about adolescents' conceptualisations of violence and the factors underlying

DOI: 10.1057/9781137365699.0009

their views on what constitutes violence (and not) is needed in order to identify more specifically the beliefs and behaviours that must be challenged through anti-violence work. This chapter seeks to contribute to the knowledge base about young people's understandings of violence and aims to illuminate the influences shaping these views.

Young people's conceptualisations of violence

What is violence?

Male and female participants in this study expressed clear views about what constitutes violence and violence was associated with a range of behaviours. These included pushing, shouting, screaming, swearing, arguments, name-calling and jealousy, as well as more severe forms of violence, such as murder, shooting, fist-fighting, punching, child abuse, rape and kidnapping. Characterisations of violence were relatively consistent across schools and across gender. Girls and boys were equally likely to name emotional or verbal acts of aggression as violence, and were equally likely to cite fighting, the use of weapons and sexual violence as forms of violence. Name-calling and verbal abuse and non-physical bullying was identified as violence by a number of participants across the sample.

FELICITY (ST. NICHOLAS COLLEGE): Like, people chant abuse at each other.

GRACIE (SYDNEY SCHOOL FOR GIRLS): Like, if you call people names or something, or you say horrible things.

TIM (BUTTERFIELD GRAMMAR SCHOOL): A lot of name-calling and threatening things, that [sic] I think is more in schools than physical violence.

RASHIDA (FISHERGATE GIRLS SCHOOL): They don't like hit you, but they make you feel bad about yourself.

Both girls and boys also named more extreme forms of violence, involving weapons and severe physical violence, in response to the question, 'what do you think of when you hear the word "violence"?'. Answers included 'blood' (Mikey, St. Nicholas College), 'knives' (Tim, Weeping Willow Boys School), 'weapons' (Farah, Fishergate Girls School), 'knuckle dusters, pocket knives, they pull a gun out' (Mona, Fishergate Girls School). Despite existing research which indicates that girls and boys associate girls more closely with emotional bullying than physical violence (for example, Hollander, 2001; Osler, 2006), young people of both genders named a range of behaviours – including emotional, verbal and physical abuse – as examples of violence here. Participants differentiated between 'low-level' and more severe forms of violence and used the distinction to classify behaviours as violent or not. Similarly, both girls and boys referred to some forms of violence as 'messing around' or 'play-fighting'.

GRACIE (SYDNEY SCHOOL FOR GIRLS): Normally when you think of violence you think of, like, someone being really badly beaten up. You don't just think of a slap.

LAUREN (SYDNEY SCHOOL FOR GIRLS): Sometimes it's just, like, messing around.

MIKE (BUTTERFIELD GRAMMAR SCHOOL): It depends how you classify it, if it's like messing around playing, but not properly a fight so to speak.

Violence between men was viewed as a comparatively typical aspect of the 'male experience', with young men suggesting that doubts about their masculinity might be raised if they refused to take part in violence. They claimed that violence was organised to take place outside school on a regular basis and this was not overtly challenged or questioned by any of the male participants in this study; rather a sense of resignation prevailed when they discussed these instances (this is described in detail in Chapter 5). There was ambivalence expressed regarding 'schoolyard' fights; negative emotions regarding the pressure to participate in fights were countered by assertions about the excitement of watching other young men fight, or watching violence on television or in sports (and the contrasting positions were often expressed by the same boys).

When asked to respond spontaneously to associations, thoughts, images and emotions related to the word 'violence', the behaviours mentioned did not indicate that adolescents in the present study held significantly different views on what constitutes violence compared with definitions that have been used in previous research with young people (Affonso et al., 2007; Cobbina et al., 2010; Fox et al., 2013a; Fredland et al., 2005; Próspero, 2006b). However, as will be discussed below, contradictions in how the violence was perceived began to emerge, as the discussion developed around the vignettes, statements and photographs. Young people appeared, on the face of it, to conceptualise violence in line with definitions encapsulated in national surveys, such as the British Crime Survey (2010, 2011, 2012) or in the Criminal Justice Act (1988). In discussions around all of the materials used, participants unanimously

DOI: 10.1057/9781137365699.0009

named nearly all the behaviours that they were shown as constituting violence. This is significant in light of previous studies which have found that young people are resistant to naming some behaviours as violent (e.g. Burton et al., 1998). However, what was additionally significant was the fact that whilst nearly all behaviours were defined as violent, not all violent behaviours were viewed negatively. Varying reasons were given for the definition of an act or situation as 'bad', including the gender of the perpetrator, the gender of the victim, the assumed relationship between the perpetrator and the victim and the assumed dynamic of the violence (one-off, repeated, escalating), as well as the context in which the violence took place. Differences in young people's perceptions of violence also differed across the medium through which the violence was presented: vignette, statement or photograph.

Who is violent?

Both boys and girls associated violence primarily with men. Violence was carried out by men in gangs or as individuals.

EMILY (SYDNEY SCHOOL FOR GIRLS): Normally when you think about violence, you think of a male.

MAX (ST. JOHN'S SCHOOL): I sort of think of men as more violent sort of people.

TOM (BUTTERFIELD GRAMMAR SCHOOL): Men in groups.

However, a number of participants across schools in the sample and across both genders suggested that women were equally, if not *more* violent than men (discussed also in Chapter 5). During the focus group discussions, it became evident that so-called low-level violence (e.g. gentle pushing, hair-pulling, scratching) and emotional violence (e.g. name-calling and verbal abuse) were frequently associated with women, and that girls were seen as engaging frequently in these behaviours.

ALI (BUTTERFIELD GRAMMAR SCHOOL): You can have, like, women go mental with knives and stuff.

FATIMA (FISHERGATE GIRLS SCHOOL): There's always like loads of girls going around and knifing people and stuff like that, it's not just men who are violent but they focus on the men because like for years, men have been more superior, so it makes their image better in a way.

MIKE (ST. NICHOLAS COLLEGE): I think girls on their own are generally more violent than guys ... when guys have a disagreement they sort of push and there will be like, maybe the occasional gut punch or something, but when girls are violent on their own, it's like nails and all that and hair pulling.

DOI: 10.1057/9781137365699.0009

This account was particularly interesting in its incongruity with a predominant narrative about the natural/genetic predisposition of men to violence, which is explored in depth in Chapter 5. Further, a number of participants made classed assumptions about violence. For example, violence was associated with 'chavs' (Trina, Sydney School for Girls), 'young men with aggressive dogs' (Saniya, Fishergate Girls School) and 'young alcoholics' (Matt, Butterfield Grammar School). This supports previous findings that violent crime is associated primarily with disadvantaged and impoverished youth (White & Cuneen, 2006). North American research suggests that perceptions of criminal injustice also differ by social class (and race/ethnicity) (Matsueda et al., 2012). The perception of violence as a deviant behaviour was particularly dominant when it was constructed as something that was perpetrated by people at the fringes of mainstream society or individuals with particular (classed) characteristics. Participants' predominantly punitive responses to addressing violence in schools (discussed in Chapters 5 and 6) and violence by youth supported this conceptualisation of violence as a criminal or deviant behaviour (Clinard and Meier, 2011) used by certain types of individuals. There were some differences in perceptions of violent offenders across schools. In schools with a high proportion (95 per cent or more) of BME pupils, significant portions of the discussion revolved around stereotypes of Asians as violent and the frequent association of violent crime with Asian men.

Excerpt from a focus group in Fishergate Girls School:

AALIYAH: It's [spousal abuse] seen like a stereotypical thing because they're both Asian ... and everyone is probably like, 'Oh, it always happens in Asian families.'

TARA: Like, in the news, if it's an Asian person who's killed someone they'd hype it up so much and then ...

FATIMA: I think the situation would be like if a Muslim killed someone that would be in the news for, like, a month.

INTERVIEWER: Mmmm.

NEETA: They're really stereotypical and whenever they give the description [of a suspected criminal], they always say 'Asian man with this hoodie on.'

AALIYAH: It's like Muslims ...

FATIMA: Is ... Muslims are terrorists.

TARA: All Muslims are terrorists and every terrorist is a Muslim.

These participants spoke vehemently about racism towards Asian communities in particular, and negative stereotypes about Asians as

DOI: 10.1057/9781137365699.0009

particularly violent and/or as terrorists. They held a perception of being positioned as outsiders and suggested that violence was perpetrated against their communities, rather than by members of them.

Place and space

Existing research on public perceptions of violence suggest that the setting in which violence occurs, as well as the perceived or actual characteristics of the victim in particular (such as appearance or behaviour) influences definitions of violence, as well as perceptions of the severity of violence (Tjaden and Thoennes, 2000; Worden & Carlson, 2005). Violence carried out in 'private', in contexts which appeared to depict the home, were commented on by some young people as being 'worse' than other forms of violence discussed. They frequently noted that the home is somewhere you should expect to feel safe.

BEN (BUTTERFIELD GRAMMAR SCHOOL) [COMPARING TWO PHOTOGRAPHS OF PHYSICAL VIOLENCE, WHERE ONE DEPICTS DOMESTIC VIOLENCE BY A MAN TOWARDS A WOMAN, AND THE OTHER DEPICTS NON-PARTNER VIOLENCE BETWEEN TWO MEN]: I think that one's [male violence towards woman] a lot worse because it looks like they are actually in a relationship so they should feel safe and it looks like they are in some sort of house and you should feel safe in your house whereas if you go on a street somewhere maybe you are more aware and if at home you are getting hit then I think that's a lot worse.

By contrast, violence perpetrated in public settings was discussed in a more voyeuristic style, commenting on the material features of the setting, and physical characteristics of the principal characters as well as of other people in the photograph if they were depicted.

Excerpt from St Nicholas College focus group discussion about a photograph of non-partner violence between two men (public setting).

INTERVIEWER: It's an interesting point. So what about this picture here?
JOSH: Is it two men?
SAM: Is it, is it two men, is it two men?
INTERVIEWER: Yeah.
SAM: Yeah.
INTERVIEWER: Can you see….
JOSH: Some type of parents if it's like a dad, two dads and some dads can be very protective of their kids and if say a football match and there were the dad's son goes and hurts the other dad's mmm son and the dad goes, "oh yeah nice tackle, nice" and the other dad just doesn't like that.

DOI: 10.1057/9781137365699.0009

INTERVIEWER: Do you think it might be two protective dads fighting over their....

FELICITY: It's like they're a load of tourists.

SONJA: Looks like they're like they're different races as well.

Previous research has shown that when violence is perpetrated 'in private', victim-blaming is prevalent (Worden & Carlson, 2005) and female victims are perceived as inviting abuse or provoking violence towards them through 'inappropriate' behaviour, for example, infidelity (Burton et al., 1998). Despite the perception that violence in the home was 'worse' than violence experienced in public, victim-blaming also emerged as a theme in young people's narratives in the YPV study. Participants invoked discourses around failure to conform to expected behaviours as an explanation for violence used by men and women. Women might be narrated as deserving of violence due to their failure to comply with a request by their (male) partner. Boys or young men were narrated as deserving of violence, for example, if they were unfaithful to their girlfriend (Chapter 5).

A distinction between these two forms of victim-blaming could be clearly identified, yet this was not closely linked to the context of the violence. Assumptions were made about particular gender behaviours of perpetrators in narratives about violence against women. Violence towards a woman might be used because a man would lose his temper more easily if a woman did not do what she was asked to do, or he might use violence because being rejected by a woman would be viewed as embarrassing or shameful.

Excerpt from a focus group discussion in Sydney School for Girls about a photograph of a man threatening a woman with physical violence (holding her by her hair and leaning over her in an aggressive manner):

LEAH: Are they on a roof?

INTERVIEWER: I don't know, that looks like, it looks like a riverbank or something doesn't it a bit.

LINDSAY: Maybe they was in an argument.

EMILY: Yeah and she'd done something wrong.

INTERVIEWER: Mmm you think she might have done something wrong?

LEAH: Because like sometimes, if like, if a boy does something and you laugh at him he has go at you or something. I don't know if he's done something stupid and he don't realise it's stupid and you laugh at him.

INTERVIEWER: Mmm. So do you think that's what might have happened there?

LEAH: Yeah.

DOI: 10.1057/9781137365699.0009

INTERVIEWER: So is that what you think like if a boy has a go at you for doing something, coz you laugh at him when he's done something stupid, is that the kind of thing he would do, do you reckon?

LAUREN: Yeah.

When young people justified women's violence towards men, they did not invoke narratives about expected gender behaviours for women or men, for example, that a woman would be more likely to be jealous or a man should protect or honour his (female) partner. Rather, the victim-blaming was done within a framework of 'fairness'.

Excerpt from a focus group discussion in Butterfield Grammar School about a vignette in which a girl slaps her boyfriend because of suspected infidelity.

GEORGE: I think it's not rare.

MATT: No that's like.

INTERVIEWER: Is that a common occurrence?

GEORGE: Yeah yeah definitely.

MATT: Yeah.

INTERVIEWER: Oh right have you guys seen it happen?

BEN: I haven't seen it.

MATT: Mmm I have yeah, it's quite funny.

GEORGE: Not when you're like the boy.

MATT: No not when you are on the receiving end.

GEORGE: Yeah yeah.

INTERVIEWER: Right okay so you think that's quite funny that mmm that you know she would slap him.

MATT: Well he deserves it.

GEORGE: Well yeah he does you can't go.

BEN: He does.

GEORGE: You can't go kissing other girls when you are going out with a different girl, that's just not on.

Gender matters

Violence by men towards men

Overall, young people were more likely to view violence in the home as unacceptable than they were violence perpetrated in a public setting, but much of this may have been mediated by the differing gender dynamics of these forms of violence. Young people's perceptions of violence were heavily influenced by the gender of the perpetrator and the victim, respectively. Male-on-male (non-partner) violence could be

DOI: 10.1057/9781137365699.0009

conceptualised as existing on a continuum (Kelly, 1988), ranging from 'arm-punching' in the school corridors, to homophobic bullying, and physical violence in and outside school grounds. Male-on-male violence was named as 'violence' but was not overtly discussed as a negative behaviour or experience. Narratives about violence between men were either explained as deliberate (and reasonable) responses to particular scenarios, or as revolving around 'serious' matters only, or they were couched in terms of needing to appear 'masculine'.

When male-on-male violence was narrated as a chosen behaviour in response to provocation, this often included notions of defending 'one's own', in terms of territory, property or family. Men's violence was viewed as a reasonable response in relation to protecting female family members in particular:

TARA (ST. NICHOLAS COLLEGE): [in response to photo of one man hitting another man]. Maybe he talks to that guy's daughter about something and he doesn't like it, or maybe his wife.

FAISAL (WEEPING WILLOW BOYS SCHOOL): [in response to photo of a man hitting a man] He must have stolen his woman.

MATT (BUTTERFIELD GRAMMAR SCHOOL): [in response to photo of man being physically threatened by another man] He probably stole something from him.

There was a perception among participants of both genders that violence between men was enacted only in relation to matters of importance or seriousness. Unlike violence that was used by women (in relation to other women and men) and which was seen as an expression of irrationality or used over trivial matters, male-on-male violence was perceived as being used when necessary – and was therefore not viewed negatively.

BEN (BUTTERFIELD GRAMMAR SCHOOL): I think it's still got to be quite a big thing for a guy to hit a guy, it's not just like very often.

JOSH (ST. NICHOLAS COLLEGE): [in response to photo of man hitting man] You wouldn't hit someone just for no reason.

AISHA (FISHERGATE GIRLS SCHOOL): [in response to photo of man hitting man] It's something major... when men and men fight, it's like, they fight about more serious...I think it's something major, I think the cause to that is something really major.

IAN (ST. JOHN'S SCHOOL): [in response to photo of man hitting a man] I don't like fighting at any time... but if there is a just reason for like, he's done something so bad you can understand why he's angry.

DOI: 10.1057/9781137365699.0009

The notion that reason and rationality determined violence between men, whereas (uncontrolled) emotion dictated women's use of violence was dominant in young people's narratives. On the one hand, this perception reflected a wider characterisation of men as rational beings and of women as 'silly' and emotional (for example, Hollander, 2001). Conversely, this view conflicted with a pervasive understanding of men's violence as rooted in their biology or genes – a 'they can't help it' narrative.

Finally, male-on-male violence was viewed as a necessary means for demonstrating masculinity. Some young men adopted an ambivalent position from which they expressed reluctance about engaging in violence, yet conceded that failure to participate in fights (or to encourage them at least) would lead to identification as not-appropriately-masculine. Further, there was a common perception that it was difficult to escape violence, even though hints at the influence of upbringing and the possibility of self-restraint were made.

Excerpt from a focus group discussion in Butterfield Grammar School:

ANDY: Oh, it's just the idea of a fight kind of scares me a little actually ... it's all in nature isn't it, like, I mean throughout the animal kingdom, it's always males who fight over the female.

MATTHEW: It's just men, it's in men's nature to attack other men, but not women, that's why it's wrong ... it's just that violence that just isn't needed is really immature and someone should be able to hold, keep themselves from attacking someone, however angry or sad or whatever they feel ...

Excerpt from a focus group discussion in Weeping Willow Boys School discussing a photograph in which a man has punched another man:

ASIF: I think that's natural for men really.

TARUN: To fight, it's not that rare to see men fight.

ASIF: Yeah.

FAISAL: They fight over anything.

ASIF: The fact they are both the same ... they are the same sex, they are both male, so I think it's right for them both to fight really.

INTERVIEWER: What were you going to say, Tarun?

TARUN: It's natural for men to take anger out on each other, but on a woman it's a different thing.

INTERVIEWER: So, when you say natural, do you mean ...

TARUN: It's just that boys, once they grow up, they are surrounded in, I don't know, they are surrounded in this area where loads of boys fight and they just learn.

DOI: 10.1057/9781137365699.0009

Violence by men towards women

Participants in this study unanimously stated that male violence towards women was wrong as an initial response to any of the materials depicting verbal or physical violence or threatening behaviour by a man against a woman. Young people invoked discourses of rationality and moral superiority in arguing that a man should 'know better' and should therefore refrain from using violence. In fact, using violence towards a woman was constituted as a non-masculine behaviour by several young men in this study; the use of violence indicated a lack of control or reason that was associated with femininity or homosexuality.

KHURRAM (WEEPING WILLOW BOYS SCHOOL): Hitting a girl, they'd probably like call him a sissy.

NEETA (FISHERGATE GIRLS SCHOOL): Since primary school, ever since you were small, if you hit like, if a boy hit a girl they would call him a sissy.

STUART (ST. NICHOLAS COLLEGE): It's gay for a man to slap a woman... I mean, it's a bit camp.

BEN (BUTTERFIELD GRAMMAR SCHOOL): He will just, like, lose all, like mmm, if you hit a woman, it's like not socially acceptable, you just lose all pride and dignity and stuff.

Further, narratives of men-as-protectors were drawn on to suggest that men's violence against women was particularly unacceptable because women (and children) relied on men for safety and protection from other men.

Excerpt from a focus group discussion in Butterfield Grammar School about the differences between men's violence towards women and women being violent towards men:

MATT: Well yeah it's not, I am not saying it's right for women to be violent towards men but it's just generally perceived that mmm that it's more okay than a man hurting a woman.

GREG: I think males and females have different roles in society and things they have different you know what they should and shouldn't do so I think that's a factor but maybe if an alien was looking at it he would think you know there's no difference but since it's been like ingrained in to us that they are different roles.

INTERVIEWER: Mmm in which way do you think they have different roles?

GREG: Well men are supposed to be the big tough ones who care for their family and then hurting them you know it's not doing their job and women are supposed to be the ones who like you know nurture the child and it's just... I

DOI: 10.1057/9781137365699.0009

don't think it's because of that, that men are supposed to care for them, they shouldn't hit them.

Men who used violence towards women were thus constructed as possessing little control and as being morally inferior to men who were able to rise above their emotions and respond differently (this might entail violence towards someone or something else, as long as it was not directed towards the woman in question).

LINDSAY (SYDNEY SCHOOL FOR GIRLS): It seems worse a man hitting a woman, because men are meant to ... be all big and macho and nothing can hurt them or make them upset or anything, so ...

NICK (ST. JOHN'S SCHOOL): Or, like, mmm if she has been cheating and that, like, might go to the person who she has been cheating with ... and maybe sort of verbally abuse him, or not abuse him ... but maybe punch or slap him.

CHRIS (BUTTERFIELD GRAMMAR SCHOOL): You wouldn't expect him to hit her [if she cheated on him], you would leave and hit the car.

Whilst seemingly progressive in the rejection of male violence towards women, this narrative of chivalry and male rationality might actually be viewed as serving to perpetuate expectations of men (even boys) as calm, reasoned and emotionally mature, and (in opposition) women as emotional, irrational and hysterical (Sundaram, 2010). Contradictions to this perspective did emerge as focus group discussions developed, and as violence was addressed in different forms/formats. The strong intolerance of men's violences against women that was expressed in initial stages of the discussions appeared to shift, dilute and be retracted as participants considered the contexts in which violence might occur and constructed stories about the static scenarios they were presented with. This will be more fully discussed in sections below.

Violence by women towards men

Women's or girls' violence towards men or boys was almost never viewed negatively, even when the behaviour itself might be named as 'violent'. In the vast majority of focus groups across all schools, violence perpetrated by girls/women against boys/men was viewed as deserved, acceptable, necessary or even comical. The latter perception was frequently attributed to the perceived triviality of violence by women (in terms of impact, as well as the matters over which violence was used) (Chapter 5). Violence used by girls was predominantly addressed in terms of relationship violence, where a girl or woman used violence, coercion or verbal abuse

DOI: 10.1057/9781137365699.0009

towards a male partner. The majority of young people in the study stated that although this did constitute violence, the behaviour was 'deserved' and 'understandable'.

ARCHIE (ST. JOHN'S SCHOOL): She should have a right to hit him because if they're in a relationship and he just goes off with another girl, then I think everyone has a right to hit.

GEORGE (BUTTERFIELD GRAMMAR SCHOOL): He deserves it, well yeah, you can't go kissing other girls when you are going out with another girl, it's just not on.

LINDSAY (SYDNEY SCHOOL FOR GIRLS): I think she has a good reason to slap him but maybe she should have approached it a bit differently... maybe just like talked it out and seeing if he was like, cause he's only saying don't worry, he's not telling her the truth.

Discourses of biology and human instinct were sometimes invoked to justify women's use of violence, just as biological urges were used to explain men's use of violence. However, in the former narrative, women's violence was not cast in harmful terms.

BEN (BUTTERFIELD GRAMMAR SCHOOL): Women, since they have like, do you when it's their time of the month they might be like more angry, so I think it's, they might have like an excuse because they may be more hormonal than men are.

MARK (ST. NICHOLAS COLLEGE): It was the right thing to do to slap him, it wasn't like, it's not the right thing to do, but it's just like a natural instinct to do because if she like loved him...

VICKY (ST. NICHOLAS COLLEGE): It's like your immediate reaction, because you're so mad at him you just go straight to slap him.

In exceptional instances some young people did state that violence by girls or women against boys or men was 'the same' as men's violence towards women. These participants noted that violence should be considered as an inappropriate reaction to the circumstances discussed whether it was perpetrated by a male or by a female.

SEAN (BUTTERFIELD GRAMMAR SCHOOL): People should be able to, adults should be able to restrain themselves, they should be mature enough not to lash out.

LEAH (SYDNEY SCHOOL FOR GIRLS): I know plenty of people that, girls are stronger than the guys they've been with... because it's the same a man hitting a woman or a woman hitting a man. It's violence all the same.

TARA (SYDNEY SCHOOL FOR GIRLS): It just seems the same because in both ways it's human instinct if they've been offended or if someone's been like, attacked

DOI: 10.1057/9781137365699.0009

in an emotional or physical way to mmm lash out. So it's the same for women and men.

An explanation for a greater acceptance of violence perpetrated by women against men might be found in participants' narratives about violence portrayed in social and conventional media which were aimed at young people. Young people in this study spoke about numerous forms of violence that take place through these media and they expressed a degree of desensitisation to and normalisation of violent behaviour on television, as well as on Facebook. Violence perpetrated by women against men was portrayed as a joke or as less serious in many televised media.

FATIMA (FISHERGATE GIRLS SCHOOL): They do it in a way where, like, they don't get punishment for what they've done, where they don't see what they've done is wrong [when women slap men on mainstream TV shows].

MADDIE (ST. NICHOLAS COLLEGE): When they show it on TV if a girl slaps a guy he just moves his cheek, but when a guy slaps a girl, she'll fall on the floor ... so that's why they say you know it's better for a girl to slap a guy because it won't hurt him as much as it hurts the woman.

Excerpt from focus group discussion in Fishergate Girls School:

YAYA: You see that [women slapping men] on like, stuff like Hannah Montana and Lizzie McGuire [laughter].

NEETA: Yeah ... like if the girl slaps the man it's fine but if the man slaps the girl it's wrong.

'Picturing' violence

Contradictions in young people's views on violence emerged when violent behaviour was discussed and depicted across different materials. The focus group discussions revolved around vignettes, statements and photographs, all of which portrayed scenarios of emotional, verbal or physical violence, and sexual harassment/coercion. Photographs in particular elicited 'storytelling' about the violence, with narratives being constructed about the assumed context of the violence and the relationship between victim and perpetrator. Forms of violence which were previously viewed very negatively were justified when represented in a different form.

Men's violence towards women was, for example, strongly rejected as unacceptable violence when it was depicted in vignettes and statements.[1] However, when male-on-female violence was depicted in photographs,[1]

DOI: 10.1057/9781137365699.0009

some young people constructed stories to justify the violence. In these accounts, the actions of the female victim explained the violence perpetrated against them, thus minimising the violence and rendering the victim partly culpable. In some instances, the behaviour was not named as violent.

VICKY (SYDNEY SCHOOL FOR GIRLS): [in response to photo of a man threatening woman] She's probably done something to hurt him [like] lied to him about something.

FATIMA (FISHERGATE GIRLS SCHOOL): [in response to photo of a man hitting woman] He might be asking her to do something again and again which she does not want to do.

RYAN (ST. JOHN'S SCHOOL): [in response to photo of a man hitting a woman] She must have done something wrong.

LAURA (SYDNEY SCHOOL FOR GIRLS): [in response to photo of a man threatening a woman] He's just grabbing her hair. He hasn't actually done anything to her yet, well you can't see.

In the vast majority of cases where violence towards women was explained or even excused, these narratives were put forward by young women. This finding is supported by previous research in the UK which suggests that adolescent girls accept abusive behaviours as 'normal' aspects of heterosexual relationships (Barter et. al 2009). An extensive body of feminist scholarship supports the notion that violence (in relationships in particular) is frequently downplayed and diminished by victims and perpetrators (Barter et al., 2009; Boonzaier, 2008; Dobash and Dobash, 1992; Hearn, 1998; Kelly, 1988; McCarry 2009, 2010). Young people may normalise violence as a relatively common aspect of heterosexual relationships and use humour and trivialising statements to construct violence as something young women simply have to put up with, or to mock young men who are seen as unable to control their jealousy or tempers (but whose violence nonetheless remains unchallenged). In the *YPV* study, they used essentialist discourses about the nature of men as particularly possessive, jealous or proud to explain violence against themselves and their friends, and seem resigned to experiencing violence within their relationships with men. In some stories constructed by young women in the present study, the victim's imagined behaviour in the scenario itself was used to discursively position her as partly deserving or responsible (also discussed in 'Place and space' earlier in this chapter). The language used implied that the victim should be *doing something* to defend herself or to prevent the violence from happening.

DOI: 10.1057/9781137365699.0009

In these narratives, the onus is on the victim to act, rather than on the perpetrator to refrain from using violence in the first place.

ALISHA: (Fishergate Girls School): [in response to photo of a man hitting woman] She doesn't look that frightened though either.

VANESSA: (St. Nicholas College): [in response to photo of a man threatening a woman] She looks used to it ... she's literally just got her hands just there, like limply she's not trying to do anything about it. It looks like she's just looking up to him like she feels inferior and she can't do anything about it.

LAURA (SYDNEY SCHOOL FOR GIRLS): [in response to photo of a man threatening a woman] If she wasn't used to it, she'd probably fight back but she's probably in the past hit him back and then it's got worse so she probably thinks oh, just sit there and do nothing.

Photographs also produced stories about violence between men, which were revelatory with regard to the factors which influence young people's characterisations of behaviours as violent and as acceptable (or not). Stories told about photographs of male-on-male violence revealed that certain expectations of men underpinned young people's views on violence as justifiable. In particular, men were obliged to protect female members of their families (and women were expected to represent and uphold male/family 'honour'). Participants' justifications of violence were thus shaped by fairly traditional notions of appropriate gender behaviour.

TARA (SYDNEY SCHOOL FOR GIRLS): [in response to photo of a man hitting another man] Maybe like that guy's daughter, he like talks to that guy's daughter about something and he doesn't like it, so, or maybe his wife.

TARIQ (WEEPING WILLOW BOYS SCHOOL): [in response to photo of a man threatening another man] His daughter or something had been messing about ... yeah, he's been messing about with his daughter or something like that.

ELLORA (FISHERGATE GIRLS SCHOOL): [in response to photo of a man hitting another man] Maybe his wife's been, like, with the other guy.

MATT (BUTTERFIELD GRAMMAR SCHOOL): [in response to photo of a man hitting another man] [Maybe he is] threatening his wife or something.

The use of photographs was incredibly useful for stimulating spontaneous discussion during which participants constructed stories about violence depicted in the photographs themselves, and which exposed the salient factors which influence young people's views of certain behaviours as violent/negative or not. Allen (2011) notes that photographs may be imbued with additional or differential meaning that may or may not have been intended by the photographer. Photographs themselves may

DOI: 10.1057/9781137365699.0009

therefore represent a realist account or 'truth' about violence, but may also be used to explore how young people themselves create meaning about violence. Taken quite apart from the material act(s) of violence depicted in the photographs, young people's narratives could be viewed as constitutive of understandings of violence and gender in themselves (Allen, 2011; Foucault, 1976).

Conclusions

This chapter has analysed the ways in which young people define and characterise violence. It has explored how characterisations of violence offered by participants in this study may differ from those used in previous research, and particularly in research which has not used youth-informed definitions of violence. A particular focus of this chapter was to investigate young people's views on different forms of violence, for example, men's violences towards men versus men's violences towards women, and to unpick the factors which influence their reading of some behaviours as violent and others as acceptable. The analysis revealed that young people may name a range of behaviours as violent, but may nonetheless be accepting of them. This finding has important implications for violence prevention; young people do not appear to misrecognise violence, but they do seem reluctant to reject all forms of violence. This suggests that efforts may not need to be concentrated on teaching young people what violence *is*, so much as challenging the factors which lead them to accept or justify some forms of violence.

Young people distinguished between different forms of violence, depending on the gender of victims and perpetrators, and the presumed context in which the violence was occurring. Violence between men was named as 'violence', but was nonetheless accepted by the majority of participants across schools. While young people did not see male violence as so 'normal' as to not describe it as violence, they did construct a range of explanations for this behaviour which characterised it as understandable and, sometimes, as necessary. On the other hand, men's violence towards women was immediately and nearly unanimously rejected by participants across all schools. Narratives around men as protectors and as inherently rational beings were used to deride perpetrators of violence as uncontrolled and not 'real men'. Women's violence towards men was named as violence, but was not perceived as harmful, threatening or

DOI: 10.1057/9781137365699.0009

serious. Indeed, in many cases, it was viewed as a deserved response to unacceptable behaviour on the part of the male victim. Underpinning all these narratives were clear and consistent expectations around appropriate gender behaviour. In other words, explanations provided to construct violence as understandable, unacceptable, necessary or deserved were based on young people's expectations of 'normal' male and female behaviour.

This became even clearer when stories about violence portrayed in photographs were analysed. Contradictions existed in young people's views on violence, such that forms of violence which were rejected in principle were actually accepted when stories around context and relationships between victims and perpetrators were constructed. The findings indicate that young people have a fairly clear idea of what violence 'looks like', but that it may be justified or accepted if the 'circumstances are right'. The findings discussed here strongly suggest that efforts should be focused on addressing factors underpinning their tolerance of violence, as well as continuing work to raise awareness of young people about different forms of violence. In Chapter 5, attention will be paid to the ways in which they actually assert their expectations for gender behaviour through their justifications of violent behaviour.

Note

1 In photographs, violence was portrayed either as physical violence or as threatening behaviour.

DOI: 10.1057/9781137365699.0009

5

Asserting Gender through Narratives about Violence

Abstract: *This chapter explores the second central theme of the* Young People and Violence *study, focusing specifically on the way in which young people make claims about gender through their narratives about violence. It is argued that views on violence are not only reflective of particular (and hegemonic) expectations of gender, but that assertions about normative gender behaviour and expectations are made in young people's discourses of violence. The findings presented in this chapter represent a distinctive analysis of gender and violence, and indicate that gender should be prioritised as fundamental to educating young people about – and preventing – violence.*

Sundaram, Vanita. *Preventing Youth Violence: Rethinking the Role of Gender in Schools.* Basingstoke: Palgrave Macmillan, 2014. DOI: 10.1057/9781137365699.0010.

DOI: 10.1057/9781137365699.0010

Introduction

This chapter analyses young people's narratives about violence, focusing in particular on the ways in which they assert gender expectations and norms through their talk about violence. Central questions around young people's conceptualisations of violence are addressed in this chapter and interactions between their characterisations of violence and their expectations for gender behaviour are explored. Other analyses have understood attitudes to violence as reflecting gender stereotypes held by young people (LaCasse and Mendelson, 2007; O'Donnell and Sharpe, 2000; Mac an Ghaill, 1994). This chapter discusses how gender norms are actively *asserted* in young people's talk about violence. Three distinct narratives about violence are explored to discuss how young people uphold expectations for gender behaviour: violence as unacceptable/acceptable, undeserved/deserved and unpreventable/preventable. This analysis is considered in terms of the way young people characterise violence, as well as how we might develop initiatives to influence their attitudes towards violence. These findings also help contextualise young people's varying definitions of violence according to context, perpetrator and victim gender and assumed relationships (presented in Chapter 4).

Gender expectations are simultaneously explicit (hyper-visible) (Krusemark, 2012) and implicit (invisible) in young people's stories about violence. It will be argued that both forms of narrative can be understood as active constructions of gender norms, even when references to gender are not overt in adolescents' characterisations of violence. The analysis draws on a rich body of evidence on narratives about violence and gender attitudes, focusing on key issues including adolescents' acceptance of and justifications for relationship violence (Barter et al., 2009; McCarry, 2010; Sears et al., 2006), gender attitudes and perceptions of violent offenders (Mitchell et al., 2009) and the intersection between seemingly benevolent attitudes towards women and espousal of hegemonic masculinity (Yamawaki, 2007). Lastly, the chapter will consider the implications of these findings for educators and professionals working in youth violence prevention. The theoretical and practical transformatory potential of the findings will be explored.

DOI: 10.1057/9781137365699.0010

What do we know already?

Important work has been done to explore the ways in which people construct themselves (and others) in their spoken stories about violence (Anderson and Umberson, 2001; Cobbina et al., 2010; Hollander, 2001; Myrttinen, 2004). Language used to describe interpersonal violence, as well as state-sponsored violence such as war (Enloe, 2007), has been shown to reflect and constitute gender difference. Boonzaier (2008) has argued that female victims of violence and male perpetrators of violence do not simply tell stories about their relationship experiences, but construct subjectivity through these narratives. Women victims of violence can simultaneously construct themselves as passive and helpless in their narratives, while reclaiming agency as they recount their journeys to ending violence towards them. Male perpetrators of violence resisted the negative 'branding' and constructed themselves positively as reformed individuals. Some even discursively produced themselves as non-violent (Boonzaier, 2008, p.190). Narratives about 'masculinised' women and emasculated men also served to reduce the culpability of the perpetrator and to justify and explain relationship violence. In the present study, young people similarly narrated perpetrators as 'victims' of frustration and pent-up emotions that they had no alternative outlets for (O'Neill, 1998). By constructing the perpetrator as 'wounded' (Boonzaier, 2008, p.192), violence can be excused. The role of expected gender behaviour in these constructions of emasculated or aggrieved men and therefore, narratives about justifiable or understandable violence warrants further exploration.

Durfee (2011) has analysed the ways in which male victims of domestic violence talk about their experiences of victimisation while upholding an appropriately masculine identity. She argues that men's narratives of victimisation reference notions of strategy, tactics and 'masculine coolness' (Durfee, 2011, p.319) in response to the violence, to avoid being labelled as helpless, passive victims. Hegemonic masculinity shapes these narratives and thus enables male victims to construct themselves as in control and powerful, despite being victimised. Other studies have shown that male victims of abuse minimise their injuries and are fearful that their disclosure of the violence will make them appear less masculine (Anderson, 2005; Eckstein, 2009; Migliaccio, 2001 as cited in Durfee, 2011). This narrative strategy constructs the violence as 'wrong' and as 'harmful' but not as stereotypically victimising.

DOI: 10.1057/9781137365699.0010

Children's and young people's talk about violence

A growing body of research has analysed the ways in which children and young people narrate violence in gendered terms. It has been argued that children's narratives may be revelatory in exposing not only the ways in which children absorb the culture on which they are commenting, but the ways in which they may manipulate or transform that culture (Miller et al., 2007 as cited in Walton et al., 2009, p.385). Particular attention has been paid to the way in which perpetrator and victim gender and contextual factors shape children's accounts of violence. Andersson (2008, p.155) has reported on the way in which expectations of appropriately masculine behaviour may be adhered to in claims made about how, when and whom it is acceptable to fight. For example, fighting men who are smaller than the perpetrator would suggest cowardice which renders it impossible to maintain masculinity (Hearn and Whitehead, 2006). A number of authors (Andersson, 2008; Barter et al., 2009; Hearn, 1998; Sears et al., 2006; Walton et al., 2009) have thus analysed the way in which young men in particular may discursively portray themselves as morally superior, in terms of being 'the better man' or a 'hero' in their accounts of doing, receiving or resisting violence, in order to maintain a successful masculine identity. This portrayal evades negative identification as simply a perpetrator or a coward if violence is rejected or received passively (and the myriad of subject positions in between). In doing so, he is able to frame his own behaviour as not-violent, but rather, being used in defence of himself or others.

Cobbina et al. (2010) found that young African–American males constructed male violence as necessary to uphold masculinity in a number of ways, including in response to a physical provocation, to avoid being taken advantage of, and to protect loved ones. This finding was confirmed in the *YPV* study (and others, including Yamawaki (2007)). Violence which is used to defend one's honour in response to a challenge, and to protect female family members particularly, could be discursively cast as acceptable or understandable violence. Not responding to these scenarios with violence or aggression would lead to potential labelling as weak or 'a wuss' and normative gender expectations would not be fulfilled. Further, Cobbina et al. (2010, p.612) and Hollander (2001) have found that violence perpetrated by women (predominantly conceptualised as being done to other women) is narrated as less dangerous, more emotionally based and about 'little, girly' issues, such

DOI: 10.1057/9781137365699.0010

as boyfriends, popularity and friendship groups. Male violence was most frequently described as being about serious issues, such as respect, honour and pride. The link between gendered discourses in popular culture and characterisations of violence among youth has also been analysed (Hernandez et al., 2012). The depiction of violence as being about respect, maintaining reputation and demonstrating toughness for young men in hip-hop songs shaped young people's understandings of what constituted violence and when it was acceptable to use violence. Young people's conceptions of violence were additionally influenced by their notions of gender roles (reinforced by the ideals portrayed through hip-hop music), including the perception that men should be 'in control, dominating and powerful' (Hernandez et al., 2012, p.595).

The role of gender expectations in shaping narratives about violence appears to be salient across cultures. Sommer et al. (2013) have shown that teenage boys in Tanzania also refer to deeply entrenched expectations around 'masculine' behaviour to contextualise, explain and rationalise interpersonal violence. Domestic violence was thus justified when a woman was seen to have threatened her husband's position in the household and the community, by undermining his authority or showing disrespect. Similarly, assumptions about men's naturally stronger sex drive and beliefs around women's sexual purity were used to rationalise sexual violence towards women who transgressed these norms and thus became too much of a temptation for men. Similar findings have been reported in the UK and North American literature (for example, Barter et al., 2009; McCarry 2009, 2010; Sears et al., 2006).

These studies have provided great insight into the ways in which gender expectations are reflected in understandings of violence in varying populations, which include non-offenders, domestic violence perpetrators and youth involved in criminal behaviour. This book seeks to build on this body of evidence by exploring young people's discourses about violence, with a view to generating knowledge about specific issues that should be considered in targeting violence prevention aimed at teenagers. The *YPV* study was, perhaps, novel in its desire to understand how young people characterise violence more generally, and to explore the cross-cutting role of gender norms in shaping their understandings of different forms of violence. This is significant in terms of viewing violence prevention as necessarily holistic in its approach; the gender norms underlying all forms of violence must be addressed in seeking to prevent specific forms of violence (including relationship violence or

DOI: 10.1057/9781137365699.0010

gang violence, for example). The study incorporated several perspectives that have been suggested for future research in existing literature. This included the inclusion of boys' and girls' perspectives on violence, the use of qualitative methods and analyses to probe youth understandings of violence, and an exploration of the link between gender attitudes and potential risk for becoming a perpetrator or a victim of violence (Hernandez et al., 2012, p.603).

The importance of letting children and young people describe their experiences of aggression or violence in their own terms has been noted. Previous research has focussed on understanding how gendered identities influence accounts of violence, without a specific emphasis on how this may inform youth-oriented violence prevention. They have nonetheless had an important focus on gender differences in interpretations of violence, types of violence girls and boys recount, justifications made for violence, and moral judgements on violence. It is argued that young people's talk does not merely reflect gender norms of which they may or may not be consciously aware, but it is a means by which young people assert and produce their expectations for gender behaviour.

Talk, violence and gender

Violence as un/acceptable

Unacceptable violence

Gender norms were asserted in relation to the characterisation of violence as varyingly acceptable and unacceptable. Notions of gender-appropriate behaviour (and this implied positive and negative behaviours that were seen as 'normal' for either gender) were told in young people's stories about different forms of violence. An unanticipated finding was that even when ostensibly benevolent attitudes were expressed regarding gender roles (Yamawaki, 2007), these drew on normative and fairly rigid understandings of appropriate gender behaviour.

One form of violence which was nearly unanimously narrated as 'unacceptable' was men's violence towards women. In response to vignettes and statements about sexual coercion and physical violence, young people unanimously identified the male perpetrator as being in the wrong and very strongly asserted that the behaviour should stop and was unacceptable.

DOI: 10.1057/9781137365699.0010

ERIC (ST. NICHOLAS COLLEGE): The man should be the bigger man, he should just leave it.

MOHAMMED (WEEPING WILLOW BOYS SCHOOL): [in response to vignette about sexual coercion] He should leave her alone ... wait until she's ready.

TIMOTHY (ST. JOHN'S SCHOOL): It's naughty [to hit a woman].

Young men in particular were vocal about the unacceptability of violence perpetrated by men towards women. However, they were less articulate about the reasons for why they thought this was the case. Many of the young men narrated this in terms of 'a sense' or 'intuition' that violence towards women was wrong, but did (or could) not analyse violence towards women in terms of gender, control or abuse of power. As Yassin (Weeping Willow Boys School) said 'it's a thing that we know but we can't put into words.' James (Butterfield Grammar School) corroborated this, stating 'men aren't allowed to hit women and that's what you think.'

When probed as to what the differences between violence by men towards other men and violence by men towards women might be, young people talked about differences in size, physical power and strength. They also asserted their expectations of gendered bodies (DeFransisco and Palzcewski, 2007; Connell, 2005) in explaining these differences. So, men's violence towards women was viewed as unacceptable violence because men's bodies are strong and powerful and women's bodies are weak and vulnerable.

VICTORIA (ST. NICHOLAS COLLEGE): [in reference to a photo of a man hitting a woman] She looks really feeble, like really thin.

LARA (ST. NICHOLAS COLLEGE): [in reference to a vignette about sexual coercion] The boy could walk away from it, but if the girl walks away from the boy, they would like grab her back.

This supports Hollander's (2001) finding that femininity is associated with vulnerability and masculinity with danger. Gendered notions of vulnerability were reinforced by participants, who consistently attributed fear to women depicted as victims of violence in photographs, but resistance or anger to men who were depicted in similar positions. Tariq's (Weeping Willow Boys School) position on this was typical of views expressed by others in the study in relation to male-on-male violence: 'He don't look scared, he ain't bothered, like what you're gonna do and that.'

In narrating men's violence towards women as unacceptable, young people expressed seemingly benevolent attitudes towards women. It is argued here that these attitudes were reflective of a benevolent sexism

DOI: 10.1057/9781137365699.0010

(Glick and Fiske, 1996; Abrams, Viki et al., 2003; Viki et al., 2004; Yamawaki, 2007) which was used to claim expectations of appropriate gender behaviour. Women's bodies were narrated as being in need of protection and men were ideally constructed as protectors.

Excerpt from focus group discussion in Fishergate Girls School:

ALISHA: If there is a girlfriend/boyfriend relationship something the guys don't let the girls go out.

FATIMA: They actually boss each other around. They don't let them go into town. My neighbour, she had a boyfriend. The guy did not let her go out at all.

INTERVIEWER: So the guy becomes like a parent?

ZAINAB: Yeah. Parents think that girls need protection.

GREG (BUTTERFIELD GRAMMAR SCHOOL): Men are supposed to be the big tough ones, who care for their family and then hurting them, you know, it's not doing their job ... men are supposed to care for them, they shouldn't hit [women].

'Serious' and 'silly' violence

The perceived and naturalised oppositionality of men's and women's bodies was also used by young people to argue that when men were violent (towards women and other men) it constituted a 'serious' act, whereas women's violence was non-threatening and used in relation to 'trivial' matters. Typically girls' violence was defined as emotional or verbal aggression, including bullying, isolation and 'bitchiness', for example, put-downs, gossiping and spreading rumours. This type of violence was also considered to be 'stupid' and enacted over trivial matters, unlike the violence perpetrated by boys which often revolved around honour or pride, which were seen as relatively more important matters. 'Trivial' matters included friendship groups, boyfriends and popularity. This supports existing research (Cobbina et al. 2010; Anderson and Umberson 2001) that young men characterise their own violence as dangerous and serious, whereas the violence carried out by girls (even when it is similar in form and character to that of the boys) is understood as being emotionally based, hysterical and about trivial matters. This narrative was further extended to characterise women's (and men's) attributes more generally. Women were thus narrated as being not serious, whereas discourses about men imbued their actions with gravity.

ASSAR (BUTTERFIELD GRAMMAR SCHOOL): With boys, they would only punch someone when they actually really meant to.

GEORGE (ST. JOHN'S SCHOOL): Because if a girl slaps a boy, it's usually to do with, 'oh I need a little bit of time alone, let me think about this', and if a boy slaps a girl then he knows that she has done something bad, and it means 'that's it, I don't want anything to do with you anymore'.

FATIMA (FISHERGATE GIRLS SCHOOL): When men and men fight, it's like, they fight about more serious things.

ERIC (BUTTERFIELD GRAMMAR SCHOOL): I think a man hitting a woman is a bit different to a girl hitting a man because the girl would hit him for some 'time-out' but the guy would have to be deeply, deeply upset, like, down there and it's really hurt him to have lashed out like that.

Young people thus produced normative ideals of men's and women's bodies in relation to, and in opposition to, violence by men against women. This finding illustrates that whilst young people may express ostensibly positive views in relation to women and may explicitly reject violence towards women, these views may be nevertheless be premised on normative and hegemonic cultural ideals around gender. These expectations for performances of gender (Butler, 1990) are significant to understanding young people's attitudes towards violence and their conceptualisations of violence, not least, their characterisation of men's violence towards each other (Kaufman, 1985).

Acceptable/understandable violence

Violence was contrastingly narrated as acceptable and as less violent when it was perpetrated by men against men. A prevailing gender discourse produced in relation to this view was that men must assert authority and dominance in relation to other men (Connell, 2005). Dominance might be asserted in relation to territory, romantic pursuits and defending honour or pride whether this was personal or on behalf of family (Cobbina et al., 2010).

ROB (ST. NICHOLAS COLLEGE): Men just hit each other to try and prove that they're hard, you know.

KAMAL (WEEPING WILLOW BOYS SCHOOL): The most common factor of boys fighting here is for insulting families.

SELINA (SYDNEY SCHOOL FOR GIRLS): He [my brother] would not let anyone say anything to me or my big sister and if they do, they just go and hit them.

Masculinity might then be achieved through acts of violence towards other men (Hearn, 2012). It is argued here that expectations of appropriately masculine behaviour were produced through the particular ways in which men's violence against men is characterised.

A further dimension of the 'violence as un/acceptable' narrative was a subtle, but significant distinction between violence as acceptable and

DOI: 10.1057/9781137365699.0010

violence as understandable. The narrative of 'understandable' violence was used most frequently in relation to men's violence against women in specific scenarios. In these scenarios, female victims were viewed as having transgressed normative expectations for feminine behaviour within the context of heterosexual relationships. Violence towards these women was very rarely condoned but it was explained and justified through the assertion of gender norms. Women who had been unfaithful to their male partners, women who did not do what their male partners asked them to do, women who had lied to their male partners and sexual rejection of a male partner were all narrated as scenarios in which normative gender behaviour had been transgressed and violence might (understandably) be used.

MARTA (FISHERGATE GIRLS SCHOOL): If she slept with someone else, then there could be a little bit of violence, but he shouldn't take it to the extreme.

TARA (SYDNEY SCHOOL FOR GIRLS): [in response to photo of man threatening a woman] She's probably done something to hurt him [like] lied to him about something.

ISOBEL (FISHERGATE GIRLS SCHOOL): [in response to vignette in which young man forces young woman to kiss him] ... It depends on how she goes about it because if she turns him away and he's like a violent person and he feels rejected and embarrassed, then it could turn into a violent situation.

As noted in Chapter 4, in the vast majority of cases where violence towards women was narrated as 'understandable', these views were expressed by young women. Stories around the ways in which women might have behaved inappropriately in relation to expected behaviour within a relationship were primarily constructed by young women, revealing entrenched and highly policed norms around appropriately feminine behaviour. Several existing studies have shown the ways in which young women police each other's behaviour in primary and secondary school classrooms and corridors (Paechter, 2010; Read, 2011; Renold, 2006; Skelton et al., 2010). These findings suggest that young women adhere to and regulate deep-seated norms for feminine behaviour within intimate relationships also.

Violence as un/deserved

Violence and intimate relationships

The second major narrative to emerge from young people's talk about violence was that of 'violence as un/deserved'. Violence between men and women as well as between men was characterised as 'deserved' in

DOI: 10.1057/9781137365699.0010

scenarios where the victim was seen to have provoked the violence, usually by transgressing accepted and expected gender norms. There were some overlaps with the 'violence as un/acceptable' discourse, as young people frequently characterised acceptable violence as deserved violence. Thus, just as young people asserted ideals around gender behaviour to discursively construct violence as acceptable, in narrating violence as deserved (or not), statements about gender behaviour were made.

Deserved violence

The conceptualisation of violence as deserved was invoked when gender norms had been transgressed (particularly by young women), or indeed, when gender relations were being constructed through the use of violence (particularly by young men). Young people named specific examples of this, including women failing to enact expected behaviours within the context of a relationship and men having encroached on the 'territory' of other men (and this 'territory' often signified women). In response to a statement which asked participants to judge whether physical violence against a woman was acceptable following an admission of infidelity, young men and women in the study refrained from naming it as 'acceptable', but rather suggested that the victim would be deserving of the violence. Whilst they did not talk about expected behaviours of men and women in relationships with much critical awareness, their talk about the use of violence clearly delineated gender-specific expectations of women in relationships.

MARK (ST. NICHOLAS COLLEGE): [explaining why a young man in a vignette might use sexual coercion] You know, she was frigid.

FARAH (FISHERGATE GIRLS SCHOOL): If they hear things about you, and they won't even ask you... Some guys do not mind you talking to [another] guy, it's just that they are like, if you cheat on them, then obviously the guy is going to get messy.

KUMAR (WEEPING WILLOW BOYS SCHOOL): If you are boyfriend and girlfriend you, like, move on once in a while and that person's not for keeps so it's not right to hit that person. But if you are in a marriage relationship it's like that person is a part of your family – if she's been cheating it's your choice if you want to hit her or not.

Whilst young people most frequently talked about male violence as unacceptable, they rarely described it as undeserved. This distinction – or omission – in itself produces a particular story about expected gender behaviour. Young men were keenly aware that violence towards women was wrong because men were physically bigger and stronger and the imperative was on them to 'be the bigger man' (Eric, Butterfield Grammar School). Therefore, the notion that violence against women was 'undeserved' did not feature in their narratives.

Excerpt from focus group discussion about a vignette in which a young man pushes his girlfriend because of suspected infidelity (St Nicholas College):

MATT: He has the right to do it [to hit her] but he shouldn't do it because... he should be more, more mature so he just leave it and don't ever see her again.

FIONA: Yeah, because it'll hurt a woman [to be hit by a man].

It should be emphasised that young people did not draw on feminist theories about gender, power and control to construct men's violence against women as unacceptable either; rather much of their rejection of this violence was premised on gendered views of bodies, inherent characteristics of men and women, and appropriate gender roles.

It was common for young people to view violence by a woman towards a man, in response to his infidelity, as deserved. The notion that violence by women against men was not to be viewed as harmful in the same way as men's violence towards women was reinforced in this particular narrative.

ALFIE (ST. NICHOLAS COLLEGE): If a man hits a woman with like, half his power, he is obviously going to hurt her and if she hits him with half her power, slaps him, it's probably not going to do that much to him.

DECLAN (BUTTERFIELD GRAMMAR SCHOOL): [in reference to vignette about emotional abuse and physical violence] I think a slap is more, she probably wasn't trying to do him harm. I think it's more of a gesture saying leave me alone, you know like, I'm angry with you.

TOM (ST. JOHN'S SCHOOL): [in reference to statement about a woman hitting a man if he is unfaithful to her] If you are just getting your anger out with a slap [it is acceptable].

Whilst it might be suggested that a sexist double-standard was apparent in their narratives, it is argued here that gendered attributes were drawn on to construct one form of violence as harmful and unacceptable and the other as less serious and deserved. As discussed earlier in this chapter, seemingly preferential attitudes towards women might actually mask sexist views about women's bodies, behaviours and qualities. Women's bodies were not viewed as dangerous and women were viewed

DOI: 10.1057/9781137365699.0010

as overly emotional, perhaps leading them to express this through (non-threatening) violence.

Violence and men

Deserved violence

The making of masculinity, the assertion of dominance (viewed as an essential, if not valorised, aspect of manhood), the protection of 'what is *his*', were cited as (overlapping) scenarios in which the use of violence might be deserved. Participants constructed a range of stories about photographs and statements that they were presented with, which gave clues as to what they 'knew' or expected of men, and therefore enabled them to characterise the violence as 'deserved'. When violence was used in the negotiation of gender and power relations between men it was viewed as deserved, if not justified. Scenarios in which men might use deserved violence towards each other included proving toughness and demonstrating manliness, winning a fight or asserting a superior position in relation to another man and protecting female partners or family members from other men.

TALLYIA (FISHERGATE GIRLS SCHOOL): Some guy whistled at my sister and my cousin's brother realised and he gave him a black eye, it was so bad.

SAM (ST. NICHOLAS COLLEGE): I think women see it as like, if a guy cheats on a girl, he has cheated on me ... if a girl cheats on him with a guy, he sees it as, he has stolen her from me, so it's like you hit the guy that she's done it with.

MARK (BUTTERFIELD GRAMMAR SCHOOL): [in reference to photo of man hitting a man] If he cheated, like if he cheated on his wife or something then you would probably expect [one man to beat up the other].

In male-to-male scenarios of violence, men were narrated as engaging in a power 'stand-off', where violence was used to establish superiority or authority. This contrasted with narratives about men's violence towards women where men were nearly always discursively positioned as more (physically) powerful. It should be reiterated that differences, in terms of social, cultural or economic power, were not recognised between men and women.

Violence as un/preventable

The third dominant narrative which emerged about violence centred on the un/preventability of violence. Gender alternately featured explicitly or 'silently' in this discourse.

DOI: 10.1057/9781137365699.0010

The nature of men

Young people's view of violence as a natural (outcome of) behaviour among humans informed their understanding of violence as impossible, if not very difficult, to prevent. Young people stated that violence was embedded in human nature, written into our genetic makeup, and was simply a pervasive aspect of the human condition (World Health Organisation, 2002). Violence was narrated as a biological inevitability that was rooted in evolutionary and psychological evidence (Buss, 1994; Gurian, 2002).

BEN (BUTTERFIELD GRAMMAR SCHOOL): I don't know if they can stop people, because I mean, hormones are hormones and they can't change that really.

JOSH (ST. NICHOLAS COLLEGE): You can try and stop it but like there's no guarantee of actually doing and stopping it. Because most of the things in everyday life are around violence.

MATT (BUTTERFIELD GRAMMAR SCHOOL): I think do you know like how the Romans before they used to have gladiators and everything and they just, they had like a lust for violence, it's the same with all of us...

Further analysis of the conceptualisation of violence as unpreventable revealed that participants held highly gendered understandings of 'human nature'. Young people expressed views about men as more aggressive, more likely to get frustrated, driven by testosterone and to be territorial. These understandings of male psychology, behaviour and attributes enabled participants to view violence as inescapable. Masculinity itself was conceptualised as a singular, innate and static attribute that might drive some men to be violent (Mills, 2001). Whilst young people recognised that not all men were violent and they spoke about women being violent as well, they did not seem cognisant of their contradictory assertion that men (as a class) possess qualities that produce violence. A tension emerged between young people stating generalised assumptions about the qualities of 'all' men, whilst acknowledging that violence was enacted by individual men.

ALI (WEEPING WILLOW BOYS SCHOOL): I think that's the way they [boys] are ... I think boys get more frustrated at these situations than girls do.

ARTHUR (BUTTERFIELD GRAMMAR SCHOOL): [in response to a vignette about relationship violence] I think he would be more likely to go a bit violent on her than her going violent on him. I think that mainly it's because men are probably more aggressive sort of people.

RICHARD (BUTTERFIELD GRAMMAR SCHOOL): Yeah, I suppose the adrenalin in guys kind of causes anger and that generally leads to more fights, while women have lower adrenalin levels and stuff.

DOI: 10.1057/9781137365699.0010

The violence-as-natural discourse produced a naturalised link between masculinity and violent behaviour. Further, it revealed an understanding of masculinity itself as an innate and generalised attribute (or set of attributes) that belong to male bodies, and that are distinct from the qualities inherent to female bodies. A vast body of existing research demonstrates that violence is used to enact masculinity (Connell, 2005; Kaufman, 1985; Kimmel et al., 2005; Messerschmidt, 2012) and that even talk about violence can be demonstrative of masculinity (Hearn, 1998). These findings suggest that young people may also make claims about 'normal', 'natural' and expected male behaviour through their talk about violence. A number of young people (young men in particular) spoke about violence between men as a relatively regularly occurring aspect of their lives (whether as victims, perpetrators or bystanders). Whilst they did not explicitly condone violence between men, it was viewed as more acceptable and this view was premised on particular assertions about the nature of men (for example, 'Testosterone causes you to be more violent', Mikey, Butterfield Grammar School).

Culpable victims

A further aspect of the 'violence as unpreventable' narrative was the presumed culpability of victims of violence in perpetuating the cycle of violence. Victims of domestic violence, specifically, were narrated as partly responsible for the continuation of violence towards them. Their perceived failure to leave their abuser or to reject the violence being perpetrated against them was viewed as an obstacle to violence prevention.

STEPH (ST. NICHOLAS COLLEGE): How could you stop [relationship violence] because if, it depends if the woman, like wants to leave the man. But if she doesn't, if she wants to stay with him, then she'll probably just carry on getting hurt so there is nothing you can do about it.

KAMAL (WEEPING WILLOW BOYS SCHOOL): You can't stop it, and like it needs to stop, but it keeps happening, like if a person keeps ringing the police and if [the perpetrator] keeps like coming back and hitting that person, then you could tell [the victim], like, move away from that person, but if they won't...

Although this explanation of the inevitability of violence is clearly distinct from the one about the supposed nature of men, there are commonalities in terms of shifting responsibility for violence away from the perpetrator. Further, in this narrative gender is not made explicit except to name victims of violence as female. Experiences of violence, as

DOI: 10.1057/9781137365699.0010

well as the prevention of violence, are understood from an individualised perspective, overlooking or mis-recognising the gender basis of violence (Bourdieu, 1986). Gender relations were referred to in many quotes but as unproblematised/unproblematic; while some behaviours relating to expectation of boys and girls were narrated as 'bad' there appeared to be little sense that these expectations could be challenged or rejected. In this sense, gender as a social construct was not understood as problematic, or indeed useful, as an explanatory factor in analysing violence.

'A few, sick men'

A further dimension of this narrative revolved around the perceived 'victimised perpetrator'. In this framework, perpetrators of violence were viewed as victims of psycho–social difficulties, including intense and pent-up frustration, aggression caused by troubled background circumstances and potential mental illness. Whilst violence was not condoned or glorified in this narrative, it was justified or excused by discursively positioning perpetrators as casualties of psycho–social trauma.

FATIMA (FISHERGATE GIRLS SCHOOL): You should give them support, saying, ok, you have done it [been violent], it's gone now, you can't change it. You can change your future now, because everyone makes mistakes, like nobody's perfect.

CHRIS (ST. NICHOLAS COLLEGE): Some people get mood changes, they just turn angry and snap. They might have anger problems.

Violence was narrated as an individualised and pathologised phenomenon, reminiscent of historical interpretations that violence was carried out by 'a few, sick men' (Hamner and Maynard, 1987). This narrative absolved the perpetrator of responsibility by referring to their assumed psychological difficulties. Violence prevention was cast in terms of counselling and alternative modes of psycho–social support for perpetrators to express and release negative emotions which might otherwise produce violence. This discourse silenced the role of structural factors, gender norms more generally or masculinity(ies) specifically, in producing violent behaviour.

Battling (with) masculinity

However, a handful of young men did talk explicitly about the peer pressure they experienced in relation to demonstrating 'masculinity'. Violence was a key means of asserting manhood (or losing face if a fight

DOI: 10.1057/9781137365699.0010

was not won). They expressed a reluctance to engage in violence but simultaneously affirmed that they were not presented with a choice: the expectations of appropriately masculine boys dictate that they engage with violence (actively or as bystanders) and the young men in this study re-asserted these.

> TIM (BUTTERFIELD GRAMMAR SCHOOL): ... it's not the two people who fight but it's everyone [else's fault] because if you imagine you are stuck in the middle with, like, someone you hate and there is a massive circle ... there is no way of getting out and if you do walk away you will be called a pussy and things like that and you will be abused.

> ARTHUR (BUTTERFIELD GRAMMAR SCHOOL): I think if people are having a fight, no one really wants to get involved, so no one will go, oh stop, it's wrong. You just wouldn't do that because you ... would probably be seen as someone who is scared and like, a wuss, or something like that.

These views were expressed by a minority of young men, and most often, social expectations of gender behaviour did not feature in young people's narratives about 'violence as unpreventable'. Even when young people's talk about violence does not explicitly reference gender, it nevertheless produces culturally dominant meanings and expectations of gender. These expectations are so embodied, so lived out, so hyper-visible, that they become invisible to the uncritical, unquestioning eye. It could thus be argued that participants produced expectations, norms and meanings around gender through their (unconscious) erasure of gender from narratives about violence.

Prevention through punishment

The narratives about violence prevention which emerged from young people's talk focused primarily on pragmatic initiatives, which might seek to change the behaviours of individuals. Young people drew heavily on discourses of crime prevention and punishment in their talk about violence prevention. The use of police to patrol public spaces as well as to give information talks in schools was advocated by many young people across the schools in the *YPV* study. Participants were in favour of leaflets being distributed with information about prison sentences for violent behaviour, the use of harsher punishments in and out of school for the use of violence, and educational posters and courses being made available in schools. These initiatives would all help prevent violence according to the participants.

DOI: 10.1057/9781137365699.0010

CONNOR (BUTTERFIELD GRAMMAR SCHOOL): If there are police about to issue, like, proper verbal warnings and then a few times afterwards, they could like fined or something like that or just something, like, to really make them stop.

FARAH (FISHERGATE GIRLS SCHOOL): [Information could be given] about how, like, if you don't realise how violent you've been, then how far it could go.

JAMAL (WEEPING WILLOW BOYS SCHOOL): People aren't educated, like, they ain't got a course or anything against violence and they don't teach about violence.

Violent individuals were frequently pathologised, in terms of criminal or deviant behaviour and/or psychological instability, and violence was viewed as a behaviour that was carried out by individuals who were 'classed' and/as deviant (Clinard and Meier, 2011). This included alcoholics, 'thugs' and 'chavs' all of whom were cast as undesirable elements in the population and therefore the ones who were likely to engage with negative behaviours, such as violence.

Finally, a number of young people across school settings did express concern that violence prevention campaigns and initiatives were 'sexist' in their focus on male perpetrators. Some participants were keen to point out that women could be equally as violent towards their male partners as men could be towards women. Ironically, this narrative was one of the few in which gender norms and expectations were explicitly named by participants; expectations of 'manhood' were viewed as responsible for low rates of reporting of domestic violence by men (also noted in McCarry, 2009). Young people did not reflect in similar ways on barriers to reporting for female victims of violence or on how expectations for gender behaviour might produce violence against women.

LORRAINE (SYDNEY SCHOOL FOR GIRLS): But there's adverts out there and they only, like protect women. Do you know, like some men get beat up by their girlfriends all the time, but people just don't recognise it.

MIKE (ST. JOHN'S SCHOOL): There are, like, times when women are also doing the domestic violence as well, like hitting the men or mentally abusing them.

FRANK (BUTTERFIELD GRAMMAR SCHOOL): It's a hard situation because if a woman is hitting you, you can really, you just don't hit them back, so what can you do ... it's like, if a girl was to beat them up, they are just going to laugh at them, like 'you got hit by a woman'.

Some young people 'de-gendered' violence by framing it as an individualised phenomenon, a power stand-off between non-gendered subjects, rather than as a gendered means of control that is located in wider culture, structure and discourse (Dobash and Dobash 1992; Hamner and

Maynard, 1987; Kelly, 1988; Donovan et al., 2006). A minority of participants explicitly stated that violence had little to do with gender; more typical was the use of gendered language to frame violence, without an explicit recognition that this was being done.

Excerpt from focus group discussion in Butterfield Grammar School:

GEORGE: I think you are missing the whole point of the girl thing because it's not ... if I had a fight with Adam, like I am much bigger and stronger, so then if I was beating him up, I don't think people would enjoy that because it would be unfair.

INTERVIEWER: It's a power thing?

GEORGE: It's all about power, it's not about sex or anything. If the woman, if the girl is raped and then she hits him then ... if they are equally matched. If he's weaker then it's unfair and people ... will try and intervene.

A gender-blind perspective on violence is problematic in terms of imagining and developing prevention initiatives. Prevention work necessarily takes on a reactive stance if violence is imagined as being done by lone individuals and the fundamental role of gender becomes concealed. Indeed, the link between the individualisation of violence and the erasure of gender from young people's narratives became apparent when they discussed the role of schools in preventing violence, as will be discussed in Chapter 6. Other authors have pointed to the potential for misconceptions about power and control among young people, even when specific initiatives have sought to raise their awareness. Fox et al. (2014) noted that young people's interpretations of control were reduced to individuals making 'good' or 'bad' decisions within relationships (which might then lead to violence being used against them).

The perception of gender parity in domestic and other forms of interpersonal violence is one that presents a clear challenge for professionals involved in violence prevention (McCarry, 2009). A critical awareness of gender expectations does not appear to inform young people's understandings of gender differences in violence perpetration or victimisation. In some cases, hostility is expressed towards work that aims to highlight the pervasiveness of violence towards women and girls, on the basis that it underplays or overlooks the violence that is perpetrated by women towards men. The resistance to prevailing messages about interpersonal violence suggests that gender education remains fundamental, and that violence prevention work must take a less didactic and/or moralising approach with young people.

DOI: 10.1057/9781137365699.0010

Conclusions

This chapter has analysed the ways in which young people actively produce and assert meanings, expectations and norms about gender through their talk about violence. Three dominant narratives emerged from young people's discussions across the six schools in this study. These were 'violence as un/acceptable', 'violence as un/deserved' and 'violence as un/preventable'. Each of these narratives was analysed to explore how young people make meaning of gendered behaviour. This chapter suggests that talk about violence does not only reflect participants' attitudes to gender roles or their understandings of appropriate gender behaviour. I argue that these young people actively assert their expectations of gender behaviour in their narratives about violence. In their explanations, justifications, rejections and acceptance of different forms of violence, they expose the gender norms that shape their own identities, thinking and actions – in relation to more than violence alone.

Gender was not always apparent in the young people's talk. At times, there was a notable absence of gender in their stories about violence. This invisibility should not be considered as indicative of young people not living within the normative confines of gender, of course. Indeed, it is argued here, that their psychological and physical embodiment of appropriate gender behaviours is so complete that it is not identifiable by them as being 'accomplished'. It might be tempting to read the not-infrequent silence around gender in young people's narratives as evidence against the production of gender norms through talk about violence. I suggest that by internalising gender norms to such an extent that they are mis-recognised in analyses of violent behaviour, young people are actively establishing normative modes of behaviour. It is imperative that we listen for/to teenagers' assumptions about and understandings of gender even when they do not tell us about them explicitly as these meanings are vital to understanding young people's views on, and attitudes towards, violence. It is well known that those who view particular forms of violence as non-violent (e.g. slapping, pushing) will be more likely to be accepting of violence perpetration and victimisation. It is argued here that it is important to understand how gendered views on context, perpetrator and victim characteristics might influence young people's definitions of violence and subsequently, their threshold for tolerating violence.

DOI: 10.1057/9781137365699.0010

These findings suggest that it is key for schools and other stakeholders involved in developing, delivering or evaluating youth violence prevention initiatives to engage explicitly with young people's views on gender and violence and the link between the two. This may entail building in an additional stage to violence prevention: before asking young people to reject violent behaviours, we need to enable them to critically engage with and reject gender norms which underlie, enable and produce violent behaviour. For example, violence prevention curricula might seek to incorporate an entire module on gender norms and expectations before addressing violence at all, rather than simply challenging hostile gender attitudes when they emerge through young people's responses to violence (and violence prevention work). Existing initiatives have deliberately sought to influence and challenge young people's gender attitudes using a whole-school approach before attempting to educate them about violence (for example, Maxwell et al., 2010). This chapter contributes further to our knowledge about young people's views on gender and the ways in which these relate to their understandings of what constitutes violence.

DOI: 10.1057/9781137365699.0010

6
What Is the Role of Schools in Violence Prevention?

Abstract: *This chapter addresses the role of schools in youth violence prevention. It makes the case for positioning schools as a crucial partner in preventative efforts and briefly reviews existing school-based initiatives. The chapter suggests that a challenge for schools lies in engaging young people with the key messages emerging from the research literature, including the primary role of gender norms in producing conducive contexts for violence.*

Sundaram, Vanita. *Preventing Youth Violence: Rethinking the Role of Gender in Schools*. Basingstoke: Palgrave Macmillan, 2014. DOI: 10.1057/9781137365699.0011.

85

Introduction

Violence and schools have most frequently been discussed in relation
to one another in the context of violence occurring *in* schools. National
and international programmes and policies to address school violence,
violence by school-aged children and young people in schools themselves,
exist in many Anglophone countries. These strategies most often adopt a
psychological or counselling lens to preventing youth violence, focusing
on anger and aggression management, the development of skills such as
empathy and problem-solving, and bullying prevention (e.g. CDC, 2013;
Furlong et al., 2005; Brown & Winterton, 2010; Richards et al., 2008).
In these strategies, schools have been identified as important agents of
change, working in collaboration with families and the wider community, to reinforce positive behaviours in children and young people, and
to prevent aggressive behaviours from escalating.

Why schools?

More recently, schools have been identified as important actors in
preventing violence by and against young people *outside* school, as well
as in school. This has included a focus on urban gang culture, sexual
exploitation within gangs and by adults, and violence within intimate
relationships. Governmental and non-governmental organisations have
noted that schools have an especially important role to play in preventing gender-based violence against women and girls (DfE, 2012; Cerise,
2011; Maxwell et al., 2010; Nasuwt, 2009). Schools are well-positioned to
be a partner in violence prevention, not least because the vast majority
of young people in the UK attend school until the age of 16. Tutty et al.
(2005) argue that there is a strong case for making schools a key site
of violence prevention work, including the link between learning pro-
social behaviour in childhood and adolescence, and positive outcomes
in adult life, and the growing perception that schools should be a safe
and caring learning environment. The NSPCC has similarly noted that
schools are well-placed to promote non-violence, and that positive links
exist between 'better behaviour and better learning' (Varnava, 2003,
p.3). The coalition government has advocated for school-based action
to reduce and prevent VAWG in particular (Home Office, 2013), and
the role of schools in protecting and safeguarding 'at-risk' children has

DOI: 10.1057/9781137365699.0011

been emphasised (DfE, 2013a). Clear messages exist about the purpose of schools in relation to violence prevention, including the right of children to feel safe at school all the time, and the duty of schools to prevent bullying on the basis of protected characteristics (Equality Act, 2010; Home Office, 2013). Gender-based violence *in* schools has been shown to be widespread; for example, nearly a third of 16- to 18-year-old girls report experiencing unwanted sexual touching in school (EVAW, 2010). The case for positioning schools as key actors in violence prevention therefore appears evident.

School-based violence prevention

However, there is mixed evidence regarding the effectiveness of school-based violence prevention programmes. Wood et al. (2010) note that programmes based in schools can have positive effects on knowledge and protective behaviours and that some interventions have been successful in reducing violence towards current dating partners. Hale et al. (2012) similarly suggest that school-based violence prevention can be effective at reducing violence against women and girls. However, the longer-term impacts on behaviour are less clear (Wood et al., 2010) and recent evidence suggests that young people do not always grasp the complexities around gender-based violence, including issues of power, control and individual culpability (Fox et al., 2014). Historically, violence prevention work in schools has not prioritised gender as central to young people's understandings of what constitutes violence, their attitudes towards violence and their acceptance of violence. Indeed, overt resistance to a focus on gender in violence prevention among youth has been expressed by some scholars (Langinrichsen-Rohling and Capaldi, 2012). There are, however, increasing and excellent examples of projects which *have* emphasised the importance of promoting gender equality as a whole-school, cross-curricular approach in order to address youth violence (Cerise, 2011; Coy et al., 2011; DCSF, 2009; Dusenbury et al., 1997; Ellis, 2004; Hester and Westmarland, 2005; Maxwell et al., 2010). The NSPCC has also argued that it is critical to educate young people about different forms of violence and help them distinguish between 'play-fighting' and abuse of power and control (Varnava, 2003) and that this should be the case across all forms of violence (Tutty et al., 2005). Existing evidence indicates that acceptance of violence against women, in particular, is

DOI: 10.1057/9781137365699.0011

best challenged if a gendered analysis is prioritised in schools (Coy et al., 2011; Ellis, 2004; Mahony and Shaugnessy, 2007). Violence prevention should educate young people about gender socialisation in their culture and seek to destabilise thinking about fixed or static ways of being a 'man' or a 'woman' (Tutty et al., 2005). Education about gender bias and stereotyping might, of course, be equally applicable to teachers and school staff.

However, recent research suggests that adopting an overtly feminist approach to violence prevention in schools can have negative effects on male students in particular and might produce a 'backlash effect' (Fox et al., 2014; Hester & Westmarland, 2005; Tutty et al., 2005, p. 14). Violence prevention programmes have traditionally been delivered by external partners to the school, such as child protection professionals, or even former violent offenders (Tutty et al., 2005). These initiatives have enabled the uniform delivery of programme content, as well as creating safe spaces for young people to learn about potentially embarrassing or sensitive topics, which they might not feel at ease speaking with their teachers about (Tutty et al., 2005). However, they may also have diluted a gender focus in violence prevention. It has been argued more recently that it is crucial to embed non-violence education into school curricula and for teachers to deliver programme content, as part of ongoing work to develop peaceful and safe school cultures. Effective violence prevention might include non-violence as a curriculum subject in its own right and through a range of interactive teaching methods (Varnava, 2003).

Most existing prevention work has considered community context, family life and school behavioural policies as key factors to consider in understanding and addressing youth violence (Walton et al., 2009). Hale, Fox and Gadd (2012; 2014) argue that a key determinant in the success of school initiatives is the inclusion of youth perspectives on their content and delivery. The challenge remains, then, for researchers and educators to develop school initiatives that unambiguously address gender in relation to violence, but that do not disengage young men (or women) or allow claims of 'sexism' in violence prevention to flourish.

DOI: 10.1057/9781137365699.0011

7
Examining the Role of (Gender in) Schools in Preventing Youth Violence

Abstract: *This chapter addresses the significant issue of school-based violence prevention from the perspective of young people. The chapter reveals that a detailed understanding of how young people conceptualise violence is crucial to developing prevention. Young people's understandings of the causes of violence and their views on what constitutes violence are intimately bound up with their views on preventing it. The findings reveal that, on the one hand, young people hold strong views about the naturalness of violence among men and the pervasiveness of violence in 'humanity', but they also associate violence with individual psychological problems. These varying perspectives shape their thinking about the preventability of violence and the role of schools in this endeavour. A key discourse (linked to the naturalised link between men and violence) was that violence is simply unpreventable.*

Sundaram, Vanita. *Preventing Youth Violence: Rethinking the Role of Gender in Schools*. Basingstoke: Palgrave Macmillan, 2014. DOI: 10.1057/9781137365699.0012.

Introduction

This chapter analyses young people's perspectives on what can be done to prevent youth violence and, in particular, the role of schools in addressing and preventing violence among young people. It seeks to highlight the link between young people's conceptualisations of violence and their views on violence prevention. More specifically, the analysis illuminates the ways in which young people's understandings of violence as un/preventable shape their views on the role of schools in addressing violence. The chapter intends to contribute to existing knowledge on youth perspectives on violence by drawing out the connections to potential practical implications for prevention.

Two dominant narratives for understanding the role of schools in violence prevention are explored. Firstly, young people expressed the idea that schools 'won't' or 'can't' do anything to prevent violence. This view was alternatively informed by an understanding of schools as disengaged or uninterested in tackling youth violence, and the notion that violence is simply unstoppable. Secondly, young people advocated the view that schools 'could' do something and, in some cases, that schools did act to tackle youth violence. This perspective was ostensibly shaped by a view that violence is preventable and that schools should and do play a part in violence prevention. The findings are considered in relation to implications for our thinking about violence prevention, including the way in which it is conceived and situated within schools. The findings are further studied in relation to changes that might be made to practice around violence education. The notable centrality of gender to young people's discourses about violence juxtaposed with the stark absence of gender from their narratives about violence prevention deserves attention. It simultaneously reveals the entrenched, internalised and naturalised place of gender norms among young people, and the impossibility of tackling violence at the cause if these norms are not explicitly addressed and challenged.

This chapter draws together the findings from the *YPV* study (presented in Chapters 4 and 5) to consider their implications for our thinking and practice about violence prevention. Schools are explicitly located as central to preventing violence among young people and this chapter examines young people's narratives around the role of schools, highlighting areas for potential growth and engagement, as well as barriers and abiding gaps in violence prevention. The chapter surveys existing

DOI: 10.1057/9781137365699.0012

research on youth perspectives on violence prevention, focussing in particular on young people's views on the preventability of violence. It will examine the factors which have been found to be successful in terms of youth engagement with violence prevention, including peer delivery, interactive methods of teaching such as role-play and cross-curricular treatment of violence. Secondly, the chapter will seek to identify what the gaps in our existing knowledge might be and in what ways this book can contribute to the debate. It will be argued that links between young people's views on violence and implications for violence prevention have not always been clearly made. Whilst our knowledge about young people's understandings of violence grows richer, we remain less certain about their views on how violence might be prevented. Dis-junctures between their narratives about violence and their views on prevention have not frequently been examined. The chapter will analyse the narratives of young people in this regard, focussing on the ways they imagine schools to be involved in violence prevention. Finally, the chapter will specifically consider the role of sex and relationships education as a site for delivering anti-violence education.

What do we know already?

A number of studies have sought to elicit young people's views on violence prevention (Affonso et al., 2007; Fredland et al., 2005; Walker et al., 2011). These have primarily been based in the United States and have drawn on public health (Centres for Disease Control and Prevention, 2004; Fredland et al., 2005; Martsolf et al., 2012; Thornton et al., 2000; United States Department of Health and Human Services, 2001; Vagi et al., 2013) and psychological (Banyard and Cross, 2008; Bibou-Nakou et al., 2013; Dodington et al., 2012) frameworks for understanding and preventing youth violence. A comprehensive review of the existing evidence suggests that a range of risk factors are highly correlated with youth violence, including gender, drug and alcohol abuse, exposure to parental violence and violence within peer or friendship group (Vagi et al., 2013). Despite our knowledge about predictors for youth violence, and teenage relationship violence in particular, many school-based initiatives to reduce and prevent youth violence have been treatment-oriented, targeting perpetrators and victims of violence through anti-bullying, behaviour management or health-care programmes (Cooper et al., 2003; Krug et al., 1997). It has

DOI: 10.1057/9781137365699.0012

been argued that examining people's perceptions of violence and violence prevention are core aspects of designing interventions (Affonso et al., 2007) and further, that preventive interventions should seek outcomes that are considered valuable by the target population. Some studies evidence a reduction in relationship violence following school-based prevention programmes (Foshee et al., 2005; Martsolf et al., 2012), but the prevalence of youth violence (in and outside intimate relationships) remains relatively high generally speaking. The picture is further complicated by sometimes contradictory evidence regarding young people's acceptance of violence in relationships (e.g. Barter et al., 2009; Burton et al., 1998; Flood, 2007).

Existing research suggests that young people hold clear views on the themes and issues that they think violence prevention initiatives should incorporate. Evidence indicates that understanding how young people conceptualise violence is of fundamental importance to effective prevention (Affonso et al., 2007; Martsolf et al., 2012) so that myths around the causes of violence can be addressed. Further, there is a need to understand what young people think constitutes violence, given the wide-ranging spectrum of behaviours that this can encompass (Kelly, 1988), in order to challenge their acceptance of violence in different forms (Barter et al., 2009; McCarry, 2010; Próspero, 2006a). Young people state that they want to be taught about how to deal with violence, including creating safe spaces and developing mechanisms for disclosing experiences of violence (Affonso et al., 2007; Fredland et al., 2005). Adolescents also express a desire for schools to recognise that some young people experience violence in their home or community settings and that this may affect their behaviour, specifically in terms of enacting violence themselves (Affonso et al., 2007; Beran, 2009; Bibou-Nakou et al., 2013; Fredland et al., 2005; Martsolf et al., 2012; Moretti et al., 2006). School-based violence prevention might provide children and young people access to psycho–social support to assist them in recovering from, and building resilience following, home and community-based conflict (Bibou-Nakou et al., 2013). Related to this, existing research indicates that community involvement in violence prevention among youth is necessary to reinforce the messages taught in school and to support young people in resisting, challenging and rejecting violence outside school (Dodington et al., 2012; Smith et al., 1999). There is sufficient evidence to suggest that strengthening the links between school, family and community may positively influence children's engagement, achievement and behaviour with regard to

DOI: 10.1057/9781137365699.0012

violence prevention, as well as other curricular subjects (Bronfenbrenner, 1979; Connolly and Josephson, 2007; Dodington et al., 2012; Ozer, 2006). Young children express a clear view that punishments for violent behaviour should be consistent and severe in order to effectively reduce it (Affonso et al., 2007). Knowledge about 'healthy' relationships has also been identified by young people as key to recognising and challenging violence (Fredland et al., 2005). Respect, trust, problem-solving skills and consent have been named as issues for schools to address in educating young people about violence (Embry et al., 1996; Fredland et al., 2005; Martsolf et al., 2012). Teenage participants in Martsolf et al.'s (2012) research described violence prevention programmes as inappropriate and impersonal, claiming that they appeared 'blind' to the existence of teenage relationship violence and that schools should address this issue distinctly and explicitly. There is some support for the introduction of violence prevention or relationships education to be introduced at an earlier stage of schooling (primary or elementary) in recognition of the fact that some young people engage in (sexual) relationships at a young age (Martsolf et al., 2012; Maxwell et al., 2010; Smith et al., 1999).

A key barrier to engagement with violence prevention may be the didactic approach that is most frequently adopted by schools. Crucially, young people are resistant to what they perceive as being 'told what to do' (Coy, Thiara and Kelly, 2011; Stephenson et al., 2004). Young people indicate that they want to be educated about their options and be allowed to move at their own pace in terms of dealing with violence or ending violent relationships. Peer instruction and mentoring is also advocated as a successful means for engaging young people with anti-violence education (Coy et al., 2011; Martsolf et al., 2012). Young people appreciate a range of methods being used to teach about violence, including through DVDs, information in magazines which are targeted at youth, and television commercials, and teaching and learning resources must be adapted to suit the cultures and values of the people at which it is aimed (Affonso et al., 2007; Smith et al., 1999; Thornton et al., 2000). We know that young people hold strong and tangible views on violence prevention. Young people want to see greater connections between what they are taught in school and their experiences outside school, including in their families and local communities. Young people do not want to be patronised or told what to do in relation to violence, but they do want violence to be addressed, and consistently so, by schools.

DOI: 10.1057/9781137365699.0012

By analysing youth narratives about violence prevention, the YPV study highlights factors of importance to young people's understandings of violence and, thus, factors which should be addressed in order to reduce violence among young people. The data presented here evidences a powerful argument for making gender equality a whole-school priority if violence prevention is to be tackled effectively. Whilst previous work has been conducted in the UK to develop and implement whole-school gender equality education, very little work has done so on the basis of analysing young people's narratives about violence and violence prevention. Schools have a vital role to play if violence prevention is to shift from a primarily reactive model, to one that is pro-active and thereby genuinely preventative in its approach. The findings presented here strongly support the notion that school-based violence prevention should depart from an individualised approach, as entrenched social norms play a fundamental role in shaping young people's views on and acceptance of violence across a range of schools and geographical locations.

Youth perspectives on violence prevention: what can/do schools do?

Young people's views on the role of schools in preventing violence are sometimes conflicting and contradictory. They alternately present schools as powerless to stop violence and as capable of acting pro-actively to prevent it. Two dominant understandings about the role of schools in preventing violence emerged from the present study: firstly, that schools were unable to, or simply did not, do anything to prevent violence; secondly, that schools were able to, and/or they did introduce measures to prevent violence. Young people's views on whether or not schools could and should be involved in violence prevention were, perhaps not surprisingly, linked to their understandings of violence as un/preventable. When violence was conceptualised as unpreventable, schools tended to be positioned as powerless, whereas the potential for schools to respond to violence was greater when violence was understood as preventable. The majority of young people articulated a view of violence as an individual phenomenon that was frequently associated with psycho–social pathology or criminal behaviour (Chapter 5). A macro-level approach to preventing violence was therefore not always imaginable or viewed as necessary or appropriate.

DOI: 10.1057/9781137365699.0012

A further barrier to violence prevention was the lack of seriousness with which it was viewed by teachers. Young people noted that teachers had 'given up', did not see it as their responsibility to deal with violent behaviour, did not want to put themselves in potential danger by intervening in violence and preferred to punish less severe misdemeanours more harshly. However, a number of young people (albeit a minority) did express strong views that violence could be prevented and that they wanted their schools to act more pro-actively to stop violence from occurring. Young people cited a range of possibilities for schools to engage with in addressing, reducing and attempting to prevent violence. None of these avenues dealt with the gender norms and expectations that so intimately characterised their own understandings of violence.

Schools (can) do nothing to prevent violence

Data from the *YPV* study suggests that young people saw schools as doing relatively little to prevent violence, regardless of whether it was seen as preventable or not. A great number of young people in the study spoke of schools that 'won't do anything' or that simply 'can't do anything' to prevent violence. In this narrative, schools were frequently viewed as not taking violence seriously. There was an emphasis on the priorities of schools being focussed on academic achievement and organisational or administrative tasks that were viewed as aiding academic success. Young people claimed that teachers were aware of violence occurring within and beyond the school grounds, but that they frequently turned a blind eye to this behaviour or they trivialised it.

ERIK (BUTTERFIELD GRAMMAR SCHOOL): It's stupid here [at school] you get a detention for forgetting your planner but you get a verbal warning for fighting.

SUFIYA (FISHERGATE GIRLS SCHOOL): But at schools they'd be like, oh, I can't be arsed with this stuff [violence, fighting].

MATT (ST. JOHN'S SCHOOL): The schools understand that young people might be violent and they have got a really lax view on it.

Existing work on models for school-based violence prevention indicates that schools must demonstrate clear commitment to and passion for challenging violence (Maxwell et al., 2010). The trivialisation of violence by school staff may permeate pupil cultures and engender a culture of acceptance of violence among young people. Further, it may deter victims of violence from reporting their experiences to a trusted adult,

DOI: 10.1057/9781137365699.0012

including teachers, if adults within schools are viewed as uninterested or as not taking violence seriously. The finding that schools are viewed as downplaying or ignoring violence in the eyes of young people is therefore significant.

The narrative of the 'powerless' school also described schools as giving up on trying to prevent violence. Schools were viewed as being overwhelmed by the scale of violence among young people and their preventative power was therefore narrated as limited. In this discourse, young people distinguished between youth violence taking place in and out of school. Specifically, they questioned the responsibility of the school with regard to preventing out-of-school violence. There was little, if any, recognition of links between young people's experiences of family or community violence, and their attitudes to and experiences of violence in other contexts (including in school) (Connolly and Josephson, 2007; Dahlberg, 1998; Hernandez et al., 2013). Young people's views on school violence as entirely distinct from other types of violence suggest that they do not fully understand the links between different forms of violence and the ways in which violence may be (re)produced in different contexts (Humphreys et al., 2008; Kaufman, 1985).

TARIQ (WEEPING WILLOW BOYS SCHOOL): Maybe in schools you can stop it ... the teachers ... but not outside school.
SOHRAB (BUTTERFIELD GRAMMAR SCHOOL): There's so much violence around, that it would be pretty difficult [for schools] to try and stop it. It would be nice if they could but I don't think it's possible.

Young men in particular vocalised a perception that schools did not really care about preventing violence and this was particularly the case if violence occurred off school grounds and/or when the school day was over. The perception that schools take an interest in the welfare of their students only within the confines of the school itself is noteworthy in light of numerous, recent policy initiatives to adopt a multi-agency and collaborative approach to child welfare, well-being and safeguarding (Coy et al., 2011; Jago and Pearce, 2008; National Working Group, 2010; Rights of Women, 2010). Violence between pupils was narrated as happening immediately beyond the school gates and teachers were perceived as turning a blind eye to this. Some young men told stories of severe violence being perpetrated against them in their local communities and young women also spoke about their fear of violence being done towards them outside the school context. Some participants spoke

DOI: 10.1057/9781137365699.0012

of planned fights taking place immediately outside the school gates that were ignored by teachers because they were taking place after the school day had ended, and off school premises. Naturally, it is not possible to directly link young people's perceptions to views expressed by teachers or school staff. However, young people in this study appeared acutely aware of a perceived lack of interest in or sense of responsibility towards them by their schools once they had left school grounds. These findings should be considered in terms of making young people aware of comprehensive and holistic approaches to child welfare, not least in terms of their knowledge about the authorities and services that are accessible to them.

When violence was narrated as unpreventable, schools were diminished of their responsibility to prevent violence. Willing teachers were conceived of as incapable and helpless to prevent such a pervasive behaviour.

STAN (BUTTERFIELD GRAMMAR SCHOOL): I don't think there is a way in schools to put an end to it because teachers can't just watch every single [fight].

ROB (ST. JOHN'S SCHOOL): In schools, you could give them like a really bad punishment but mmm and that would probably deter them from it but I am not sure that it would completely put a stop to it.

A near-fatalistic account of violence (prevention) was given in this narrative; violence simply 'happens' and even if teachers were able to prevent or break-up a single fight within their schools, they would not be in a position to prevent subsequent violence which was bound to take place after school hours. The assumed naturalness of violence, as an inevitable aspect of the human (male) condition was used to construct it as unpreventable. Boys, in particular, were constructed as seeking out violence for revenge, to assert authority or dominance, and sometimes even for pleasure (George (Butterfield Grammar School): 'It's fun to watch ... it's kind of like an adrenalin rush in the moment, you just kind of get a buzz out of seeing two guys battling in vain, it's totally useless sometimes.') The scepticism regarding the preventative potential of schools might be reflective of a wider mistrust of institutions which are characterised by hierarchy, power differences and processes which themselves might be classed as violent (Francis and Mills, 2012). Young people's attitudes around respect, equality, power and control may therefore be shaped by the institutional culture and practices of schools themselves.

DOI: 10.1057/9781137365699.0012

Schools do something to prevent violence

The second narrative regarding the role of schools in preventing violence was that schools can, and do, develop initiatives to prevent violence. The former discourse implied that schools might be doing more than they were currently, whereas the latter described the positive actions young people felt their schools were already engaging in to reduce violence. Both viewpoints described measures that were reactive, rather than pro-active, in their approach to violence. It is argued here that reactive actions reinforce a symptom-based approach which sees violence as a phenomenon to be responded to once it has taken place. A pro-active stance would address the underlying causes of violence and would seek to prevent violence before it occurs (for example, Coy et al. (2011)). Young people's notions of violence prevention were predominantly focused on violence *response*. However, some proposed initiatives were conceived as deterrents to violent behaviour and could therefore be considered preventative in their conceptualisation.

The initiatives proposed by young people as effective in terms of preventing violence were primarily concerned with the punishment and reduction of criminal behaviour. As described in Chapter 4, young people's narratives revealed classed understandings of criminality (White and Cuneen, 2006). However, proposed solutions to violence did not reflect such classed perceptions of perpetrators. Young people focussed more generally on the merits of police-led workshops, information about prison sentences, and guest lectures by ex-offenders (Chapter 5). It is noteworthy that none of the measures proposed or described by young people addressed gender inequality. Although gender norms were both explicitly and implicitly woven into their narratives about violence, young people did not conceive of it as necessary to address gender in seeking to prevent violence.

Young people in this study had a range of suggestions for what schools could do to prevent violence and were relatively outspoken about the perceived feebleness of many school-level responses to violence, which were not viewed as reflecting a sustained commitment to prevent violence. School responses were often viewed as weak, inconsistent and as one-off reactions to isolated incidents.

VIJAY (WEEPING WILLOW BOYS SCHOOL): Teachers just tell them [a violent pair in school] off and then just sometimes like exclude them.

PATRICK (BUTTERFIELD GRAMMAR SCHOOL): Maybe harsher punishments [are needed for violence] ... punishments need to be much more severe, for example, calling their parents or suspension or something like that.

DOI: 10.1057/9781137365699.0012

TIM (ST. JOHN'S SCHOOL): If there's a really big proper fight and people are getting injured then people can get excluded and stuff, [but] where teachers split it up and they get like detention or something, it doesn't put people off fighting.

No participants spoke about existing school measures to educate young people about violence in the community and staying safe outside school. Some young people did suggest that violence prevention could be delivered in collaboration between the school and the community (Tamara (Fishergate Girls School): 'Maybe if someone could actually come and talk to them, like, say if they had a youth club thing and talk about violence.'). The majority of existing measures to prevent violence was focused on punishing the behaviour of individuals and were described as isolated actions, rather than as part of a comprehensive, whole-school approach to address, reduce and prevent violence. It should be acknowledged that no teachers were interviewed to ascertain what school initiatives might be in place that students did not mention. However, young people's narratives reveal two important findings: namely that they perceive school responses to violence as ones that tackle lone and individual behaviours, and secondly, that this perception reinforces their predominant understandings of violence as an individualised phenomenon. Young people's narratives about violence prevention – existing and proposed initiatives – did not appear to be cognisant of the roots of violence in particular (gendered) socio–cultural modes and expectations for behaviour.

The individualised view of violence stood in contradiction to young people's stated impression of the pervasiveness of violence. Participants across the schools asserted that violence was simply too widespread for schools to control, that it was so pervasive as to be natural, and that it was 'all around us' and 'unstoppable'. Thus, there appeared to be some recognition that violence was not simply perpetrated by a few individuals; however, proposed measures to prevent violence (and existing measures of which they approved) focused on changing individuals' behaviours.

The use of suspensions or exclusions was frequently mentioned by young people as a potentially effective school-level punishment for violence. The concern of participants was to enforce discipline and manage negative behaviour by changing or increasing the severity of punishments. A prevalent co-narrative to the 'discipline and punish' approach (to appropriate Foucault (1975)) was that schools could increase awareness of punishments outside the school setting as a deterrent to

DOI: 10.1057/9781137365699.0012

violence. Whilst schools were not narrated as being responsible for educating young people about violence in the community, there was support for teaching about 'real-world' examples of punishments for violent behaviour. Young people adopted the view that fear of being subjected to these punishments would act as a powerful deterrent to would-be perpetrators of violence. Proposed actions included guest lectures by local police officers, workshops led by ex-offenders to educate young people about prison life, information about the length of prison sentences for violent behaviour and involving youth club leaders to talk to young people about the consequences of violence (albeit mainly for the lives of perpetrators of violence, rather than for the victims).

WAQAS (WEEPING WILLOW BOYS SCHOOL): They did 'Prison? Me, no way' ... that was about violence and how to stop it and all that ... police officers came into our school and they were just telling us about how to prevent it and about the consequences of our actions maybe and how many years we could get in prison.

LISA (ST. NICHOLAS COLLEGE): [information] about how long you can get in prison if you get, like, found out.

ZAINAB (FISHERGATE GIRLS SCHOOL): Or if you make them feel how they would feel in that situation [if they were victimised].

An approach which appeals to fear and to a selfish motivation to avoid punishment is short-sighted and does not address the fundamental causes of violence. It might simply mirror and perpetuate existing school processes which prioritise behaviour management and discipline, and which reinforce power differentials between teachers and pupils. This approach may not only fail to prevent violence in the long-term, but may contribute to existing violent school practices (Francis and Mills, 2012). A rights-based approach in which young people are educated about respect for their own as well as other people's human rights is likely to be more sustainable in terms of effectuating behavioural change (Dusenbury et al., 1997; Ellis, 2004; Maxwell et al., 2010). This approach addresses gender inequality at its source by fundamentally influencing views on men and women, rather than attempting to change already-entrenched attitudes or behaviours as they emerge. Some young people – a minority of participants – did suggest pro-active approaches to violence prevention which were founded on educating young people about the impacts of violence on victims and which implicitly drew on a rights discourse. Rather than isolated punishments for violent behaviour, these proposed measures prioritised interactive methods for illuminating the reasons

DOI: 10.1057/9781137365699.0012

why people might resort to violence, the effects of violence for victims, awareness-raising about sources of victim support and sources of information about what constitutes violence in different contexts.

TIM (ST. JOHN'S SCHOOL): More detailed [information about] why someone would do something like that [violence].

HAMSA (WEEPING WILLOW BOYS SCHOOL): Maybe workshops, like for example, they were doing one about mmm driving you know, when you shouldn't drink and drive and they were doing like a kind of presentation, like a bit of a drama.

NOREEN (FISHERGATE GIRLS SCHOOL): If I was like a teacher teaching about it, I wouldn't make it stand out like, violence is wrong, don't do it, like make it sound real dull. I would ... be more involved than just like sitting down talking about it.

GEORGE (BUTTERFIELD GRAMMAR SCHOOL): Or maybe with you [with researcher] as like with talks like this, and like tell us about what's happening with the violence campaign and things like that so then we are aware of it.

These suggestions did, at least, offer a pro-active perspective on violence prevention. They were distinct from the predominant disciplinarian/punitive discourse and reflected a commitment to educating young people – about why perpetrators might be violent, about how victims might be supported and about the longer-term consequences of using violence. However, young people did not mention gender norms or expectations as an aspect of violence prevention, despite the fact that some young men across school settings had told stories about being pressured to engage in violence as part of a performance of masculinity (Chapter 5). Young people did not appear aware even of the possibility of challenging these norms, much less the role of education in facilitating this.

What do young people's views tell us about preventing youth violence?

Young people's narratives about violence prevention viewed schools as alternately powerless and powerful. Schools were either viewed as inactive in terms of preventing violence or as (potentially) active. Fundamentally, young people viewed schools as doing very little to prevent violence. Claims were made about the disengagement and inconsistency of individual schools' actions. A narrative analysis of young people's views

DOI: 10.1057/9781137365699.0012

on violence prevention reveals their lack of recognition and awareness of the centrality of gender in producing and reinforcing violence behaviour. It is suggested that the perceived (in)actions of schools with regard to violence serves to strengthen their blindness in relation to gender.

Even when young people proposed pro-active, preventative measures that could be taken by schools to prevent violence, it is notable that the focus of these remained gender neutral. Generic proposals to educate young people about causes of violence, impacts of violence on victims and consequences for perpetrators were made, seemingly without any awareness of the gender-specificity of violence perpetration and victimisation. The data from this study indicates, however, that gender norms and expectations are significant in shaping young people's understandings of violence. Further, notions about gender difference are crucial to their continuing acceptance of and engagement with violence, as perpetrators, victims and bystanders. Young people's understandings of violence as preventable (or not) are shaped by their perceptions of gender difference, specifically, links between understandings of masculinity and femininity, and the perpetuation of violence.

These findings indicate that gender norms are deeply entrenched, internalised, policed and reproduced by young people. Work must be done to render these norms visible to young people to enable them to engage critically with the alterable nature of these expectations. This work should enable young people to imagine different ways of being, to create a culture of acceptance and respect around alternative gender and sexual identities, behaviours and practices, and to reject the hegemony of prevalent gender norms. It is argued here that this is fundamental to (school-based) violence prevention. A rich body of evidence shows that schools are sites for the production and reproduction of gender norms, through school organisation, pupil cultures and teacher expectations (Reay, 2001; Renold, 2006; Paechter, 2010). It is therefore vital that schools play a central role in challenging these gender norms. This entails work being done with teachers as well as pupils to challenge their deeply held ideas about the nature of boys and girls and the veracity of gender difference. Excellent but relatively atypical examples of work have outlined necessary changes to organisational cultures and school curricula in order to effectuate attitudinal and behavioural change among schools staff and pupils (Coy et al., 2011; Dusenbury et al., 1997; Hester and Westmarland, 2005; Maxwell et al., 2010).

DOI: 10.1057/9781137365699.0012

The potential of sex and relationships education

Recent and increasing attention has been paid to the role of sex and relationships education (SRE) in preventing violence in the UK. In particular, the potential for SRE to tackle teenage relationship violence has been emphasised by government advisors, policy makers, curriculum developers, practitioners and activists alike (Dustin, 2013; Ofsted, 2013; Home Office, 2013; OCC, 2012; Sex Education Forum, 2013). Sex and relationships education is, of course, about more than the mechanics of sex. A growing body of research has shown that gender identities and norms play a significant mediating role in the negotiation of behaviour, including sexual practices, within relationships (Epstein et al., 2012; Holland et al., 1998; Measor et al., 2000; Renold and Ringrose, 2011; Spencer et al., 2008). As Donovan and Hester (2008, p.279) have noted, the choices young people make about sex, love and relationships are not simply individualised decisions or choices, but are shaped by beliefs and expectations around gender and sexuality in a given culture or society. Data from the current study indicates that young people view violent behaviour as a 'natural' aspect of masculine/male behaviour and that this perception is strongly internalised, and used to explain and justify male violence in (and out of) intimate relationships. Whilst gender equality work should be embedded across the school curriculum, relationship violence in particular might usefully be incorporated into SRE.

The findings reported here suggest that it is vital to address gender norms in particular, when educating young people about positive and respectful relationships. There exists a legislative framework in the UK which is supportive of schools teaching equality-based subjects (Equality Act, 2010), including gender equality and respectful, non-violent relationships between women and men (Equality and Human Rights Commission, 2010). Proposals to make gender education an aspect of SRE exist (NHS 2001; Brook 2013; EVAW 2013); however, steps for implementing this are currently located at the school or local authority level. This book does not claim to provide the definite answer about the content and delivery of youth violence prevention. It has attempted to explore young people's views on violence and to think about how violence prevention might look if we were to take account of their voices. It is my hope that the book has contributed to our understanding of some of the necessary elements of effective, youth-targeted violence prevention.

DOI: 10.1057/9781137365699.0012

References

Abrams, D., Viki, G.T., Masser, B., & Bohner, G. (2003). Perceptions of Stranger and Acquaintance Rape: The Role of Benevolent and Hostile Sexism in Victim Blame and Rape Proclivity. *Journal of Personality and Social Psychology, 84,* 111–125.

Ackard, D.M., Eisenberg, M.E., & Neumark-Stzainer, D. (2012). Associations between Dating Violence and High-Risk Sexual Behaviors among Male and Female Older Adolescents. *Journal of Child and Adolescent Trauma, 5 (4),* 344–352.

Affonso, D.D., Shibuya, J.Y., & Frueh, C.B. (2007). Talk-Story: Perspectives of Children, Parents, and Community Leaders on Community Violence in Rural Hawaii. *Public Health Nursing, 24(5),* 400–408.

Allen, L. (2009). 'Snapped': Researching the Sexual Culture of Schools Using Visual Methods. *International Journal of Qualitative Studies in Education, 22(5),* 549–561.

Allen, L. (2011). 'Picture this': Using Photo-Methods in Research on Sexualities and Schooling. *Qualitative Research, 11(5),* 487–504.

Anderson, K. L. (2005). Theorising Gender in Intimate Partner Violence Research. *Sex Roles, 52* (11/12), 853–865.

Anderson, K.L. and Umberson, D. 2001. Gendering Violence: Masculinity and Power in Men's Accounts of Domestic Violence. *Gender and Society 15(3),* 358–380.

DOI: 10.1057/9781137365699.0013

Anderson, L. A., & Whitson, S. C. (2005). Sexual Assault Education Programs: a Meta-Analytic Examination of Their Effectiveness. *Psychology of Women Quarterly, 29,* 374–388.

Andersson, K. (2008). Constructing Young Masculinity: a Case Study of Heroic Discourse on Violence. *Discourse & Society, 19(2),* 139–161.

Ausbrooks, A.R. (2010). Perceptions of Violence: A Youthful Perspective. *School Social Work Journal, 34(2),* 1–17.

Ball, B., Kerig, P. K., & Rosenbluth, B. (2009). "Like a family but better because you can actually trust each other": The Expect Respect Dating Violence Prevention Program for at-Risk Youth. *Health Promotion Practice, 10(1),* 45S–58S.

Banos Smith, M. (2011). *A Different World is Possible: Promising Practices to Prevent Violence against Women and Girls.* London: End Violence Against Women.

Banyard, V. L., & Cross, C. (2008). Consequences of Teen Dating Violence: Understanding Intervening Variables in Ecological Context. *Violence Against Women, 14(9),* 998–1013.

Barter, C., & Renold, E. (2000). 'I wanna tell you a story': The Use of Vignettes in Qualitative Research. *International Journal of Social Research Methodology, 3(4),* 307–323.

Barter, C., & Renold, E. (2002). Dilemmas in Control: Methodological Implications and Reflections of Foregrounding Children's Perspectives on Violence. In E. Stanko, & R. Lee (Eds), *Researching Violence.* London: Routledge.

Barter, C., McCarry, M., Berridge, D., &Evans, K. (2009). *Partner Exploitation and Violence in Teenage Intimate Relationships.* University of Bristol and NSPCC.

Barter, C., Renold, E., Berridge, D., & Cawson, P. (2004). *Peer Violence in Children's Residential Care.* Basingstoke: Palgrave Macmillan.

Bellis, M., Hughes, K., Perkins, C., & Bennett, A. (2012). *Protecting People, Promoting Health. a Public Health Approach to Violence Prevention for England.* North West Public Health Observatory, Centre for Public Health: Liverpool John Moores University.

Best, A. (2007). *Representing Youth: Methodological Issues in Critical Youth Studies.* New York: New York University Press.

Bibou-Nakou, I., Tsiantis, J., Assimopoulos, H., & Chatzilambou, P. (2013). Bullying/Victimization from a Family Perspective: A Qualitative Study of Secondary School Students' Views. *European Journal of Psychology of Education 28(1),* 53–71.

DOI: 10.1057/9781137365699.0013

Blumer, H. (1969). *Symbolic Interactionism: Perspective and Method.* Englewood Cliffs, NJ: Prentice-Hall.

Boonzaier, F. (2008). 'If the Man Says you Must Sit, Then you Must Sit': The Relational Construction of Woman Abuse: Gender, Subjectivity and Violence. *Feminism and Psychology, 18(2),* 183–206.

Boston Public Health Commission. (2009). *Start Strong Initiative* (http://www.bphc.org/whatwedo/violence-prevention/start-strong/Pages/Start-Strong.aspx) (Accessed 28 February 2014).

Bourdieu, P. (1986). The Forms of Capital. In J.G. Richardson (Ed.), *Handbook of Theory and Research for the Sociology of Capital* (pp. 241–258). New York: Greenwood Press.

British Educational Research Association (BERA). (2011). *Ethical Guidelines for Educational Research.* London: BERA.

Bronfenbrenner, U. (1979). *The Ecology of Human Development: Experiments by Nature and Design.* Cambridge, MA: Harvard University Press.

Brook (2013). *Brook and* fpa *Briefing on Sex and Relationships Education.* (http://www.fpa.org.uk/sites/default/files/sre-briefing-brook-fpa-march-2013.pdf) (Accessed 10 October 2013).

Brown, J., & Winterton, M. (2010). *Violence in* uk *Schools: What Is Really Happening?* Insight 1. British Educational Research Association.

Bruner, J. (1997). Labov and Waletzky: Thirty Years on. *Journal of Narrative and Life History, 7,* 61–68.

Bryman, A. (2008). *Social Research Methods* (3rd edn). Oxford: Oxford University Press.

Burton, S., Kelly, L., Kitzinger, J. & Regan, L. (1998). Young People's Attitudes Towards Violence, Sex and Relationships: A Survey and Focus Group Study. Zero Tolerance Charitable Trust, Research Report 002.

Buss, D.M. (1994). *The Evolution of Desire: Strategies of Human Mating.* New York: Basic Books.

Butler, J. (1990). *Gender Trouble. Feminism and the Subversion of Identity.* London: Routledge.

Calder, B.J. (1977). Focus Groups and the Nature of Qualitative Research. *Journal of Marketing Research, 14,* 353–364.

Cameron, D. (1998). Gender, Language and Discourse: A Review Essay. *Signs, 23(4),* 945–973.

Cameron, D. (2001). *Working with Spoken Discourse.* London: SAGE Publications.

DOI: 10.1057/9781137365699.0013

Campbell, J. C., & Dienemann, J. D. (2001). Ethical Issues in Research on Violence against Women. In C. M. Renzetti, J. L. Edleson, & R. K. Bergen (Eds), *Sourcebook on Violence against Women* (pp. 57–72). Newbury Park, CA: Sage.

Cerise, S. (2011). a *Different World Is Possible*: a *Call for Long-Term and Targeted Action to Prevent Violence against Women and Girls*. London: End Violence Against Women.

Centres for Disease Control and Prevention (CDC). (2004). *Striving to Reduce Youth Violence Everywhere: STRYVE*. (http://www.vetoviolence.cdc.gov/STRYVE) (Accessed 10 October 2013).

Chamberlain, T., George, N., Golden, S., Walker, F., & Benton, T. (2010). *Tell4us National Report*. National Foundation for Educational Research, Department for Children, Schools and Families.

Chaplin, R. Flatley, J., & Smith, K. (Eds) (2011). *Crime in England and Wales, 2010/11. Findings from the British Crime Survey and Police Recorded Crime*. Home Office Statistics.

Chapman, R.L., Buckley, M., Sheehan, M., & Shochet, I.M. (2013). Pilot Evaluation of an Adolescent Risk and Injury Prevention Programme Incorporating Curriculum and School Connectedness Components. *Health Education Research, 28 (4)*, 612–625.

Chase, S.E. (2005). Narrative Inquiry: Multiple Lenses, Approaches, Voices. In N.K. Denzin & Y.S. Lincoln (Eds), *The SAGE Handbook of Qualitative Research* (3rd edn). London: Sage Publications.

Christensen, P., & James, A. (2008). *Research with Children: Perspectives and Practices* (2nd edn). London: Routledge.

Clinard, M.B., & Meier, R.F. (2011). *Sociology of Deviant Behaviour* (14th edn). Belmont, California: Wadsworth Cengage Learning.

Cobbina, J. E., Like-Haislip, T.Z., & Miller, J. (2010). Gang Fights versus Cat Fights: Urban Young Men's Gendered Narratives of Violence. *Deviant Behaviour, 31*, 596–624.

Connell, RW. (2001). Understanding Men: Gender Sociology and the New International Research on Masculinities. *Social Thought and Research, 24 (1/2)*, 13–31.

Connell, R.W. (2002). On Hegemonic Masculinity and Violence: Response to Jefferson and Hall. *Theoretical Criminology, 6 (1)*, 89–99.

Connell, R.W. (2005). *Masculinities* (2nd edn). Cambridge: Polity Press.

Connell, R.W., & Messerschmidt, J.W. (2005). Hegemonic Masculinity: Rethinking the Concept. *Gender and Society, 19 (6)*, 829–859.

DOI: 10.1057/9781137365699.0013

Connolly, J., & Josephson, W. (2007). Aggression in Adolescent Dating Relationships: Predictors and Prevention. *The Prevention Researcher, 14*, 3–5.

Cooper, W. O., Lutenbacher, M., Faccia, K., & Hepworth, J. T. (2003). Planning of Youth Violence-Prevention Programs: Development of a Guiding Measure. *Public Health Nursing, 20(6)*, 432–439.

Coy, M., Thiara, R. K. & Kelly, L. (2011). *Boys Think Girls Are Toys? An Evaluation of the NIA Project Prevention Programme on Sexual Exploitation.* London: CWASU.

Davies, I. (2012). Teaching about Genocide. In P. Cowan & H. Maitles (Eds), *Teaching about Controversial Issues in the Classroom: Key Issues and Debates* (pp. 108–119). London: Continuum Books.

Deacon, D., Pickering, M., Golding, P., & Murdock, G. (1999). *Researching Communications: A Practical Guide to Methods in Media and Cultural Analysis.* London: Arnold Publishers.

Dahlberg, L.L. (1998). Youth Violence in the United States: Major Trends, Risk Factors, and Prevention Approaches. *American Journal of Preventive Medicine 14(4)*, 259–272.

DeFransisco, V.P., & Palzcewski, C.H. (2007). *Communicating Gender Diversity.* Thousand Oaks, CA: Sage Publications.

Denzin, L. (1997). *Interpretive Ethnography: Ethnographic Practices for the 21st Century.* Thousand Oaks, CA: Sage Publications.

Denzin, N.K., & Lincoln, Y.S. (Eds) (1998). *Strategies of Qualitative Inquiry.* Thousand Oaks, CA: Sage Publications.

Denzin, N.K., & Lincoln, Y.S. (Eds) (2005). *The SAGE Handbook of Qualitative Research* (3rd edn). London: Sage Publications.

Department for Children, Schools and Families (DCSF). (2009). *Guidance for Schools on Preventing and Responding to Sexist, Sexual and Transphobic Bullying — Safe to Learn: Embedding Anti-Bullying Work in Schools.* HM Government. Nottingham: DCSF Publications.

Department for Children, Schools and Families (DCSF). (2010a). *Response to the Violence against Women and Girls Advisory Group's Recommendations.* HM Government (DCSF-00288–2010).

Department for Children, Schools and Families (DCSF). (2010b). *Safeguarding Children and Young People Who May Be Affected by Gang Activity.* hm *Government* (DCSF-00064–2010).

Department for Communities and Local Government. (2012). *Working with Troubled Families: A Guide to the Evidence and Good Practice.* HM Government.

DOI: 10.1057/9781137365699.0013

Department for Education (DfE) (2004). Department for Education and Skills. *Every Child Matters: Change for Children*. HM Government.

Department for Education (DfE) (2012). Personal, Social, Health and Economic Education (PSHEE). HM Government. (http://www.education.gov.uk/schools/teachingandlearning/curriculum/secondary/b00198880/pshee) (Accessed 10 October 2013).

Department for Education (DfE) (2013a). *Working Together to Safeguard Children. a Guide to Inter-Agency Working to Safeguard and Promote the Welfare of Children*. HM Government.

Department for Education (DfE) (2013b). *School Census*. (http://www.education.gov.uk/researchandstatistics/stats/schoolcensus/a00208045/school-census-2013) (Accessed 15 October 2013).

DeKeseredy, W.S., & Schwartz, M.D. (2005). Masculinities and Interpersonal Violence. In M. Kimmel, J. Hearn & R.W. Connell (Eds), *The Handbook of Studies on Men and Masculinities* (pp. 353–367). London: Sage.

Dobash, R.E., & Dobash, R.P. (1992). *Women, Violence & Social Change*. Abingdon, Oxon: Routledge.

Dodington, J., Mollen, C., Woodlock, J., Hausman, A., Richmond, T.S., & Fein, J.A. (2012). Youth and Adult Perspectives on Violence Prevention Strategies: a Community-Based Participatory Study. *Journal of Community Psychology, 40*, 1022–1031.

Donovan, C. and Hester, M. (2008). 'Because she was my first girlfriend, I didn't know any different': Making the Case for Mainstreaming Same-Sex Sex/Relationship Education. *Sex Education, 8(3)*, 277–287.

Donovan, C., Hester, M., McCarry, M., & Holmes, J. (2006). *Comparing Domestic Abuse in Same-Sex and Heterosexual Relationships*. Bristol: Universities of Bristol and Sunderland.

Dublin Women's Aid. (1999). *Teenage Tolerance: The Hidden Lives of Young Irish People. a Study of Young People's Experience and Responses to Violence and Abuse*. Dublin: Women's Aid.

Durfee, A. (2011). I'm not a victim, she's an abuser: Masculinity, Victimization, and Protection Orders. *Gender & Society, 25*, 316–344.

Dusenbury, L., Falco, M., Lake, A., Brannigan, R., & Bosworth, K. (1997). Nine Critical Elements of Promising Violence Prevention Programs. *Journal of School Health, 67(10)*, 409–414.

Dustin, H. (2013). Sex Education Can Help Tackle the Abuse of Girls. So Will the Tories Commit to It? (http://www.theguardian.com/

DOI: 10.1057/9781137365699.0013

commentisfree/2012/oct/05/sex-education-child-abuse-tories) (Accessed 16 October 2013).

Eckstein, J. (2009). Exploring the Communication of Men Revealing Abuse from Female Intimate Partners. In D.D. Cahn (Ed.), *Family Violence: Communication Processes* (pp. 89–111). Albany: State University of New York Press.

Ellis, J. (2004). *Preventing Violence against Women and Girls: a Study of Educational Programmes for Children and Young People.* Final Report for WOMANKIND Worldwide. Unpublished.

Ely, G. (2004). Adolescent Dating Violence on School Campuses. *Journal of Evidence-Based Social Work, 1 (2/3),* 143–157.

Embry, D.D., Flannery, D.J., Vazsonyi, A.T., Powell, K.E., & Atha, H. (1996). Peacebuilders: A Theoretically Driven, School-Based Model for Early Violence Prevention. *American Journal Preventative Medicine, 12(5 Suppl),* 91–100.

End Violence Against Women Coalition. (2010). *Preventing Violence Against Women* (http://www.endviolenceagainstwomen.org.uk/ preventing-violence-against-women). Accessed 22 April 2014.

End Violence Against Women Coalition. (2013). 'Better Sex Education' *campaign.* (http://www.endviolenceagainstwomen.org.uk/news/111/ evaw-others-sex-education-letter-featured-in-daily-telegraph-campaign). Accessed 22 April, 2014.

Enloe, C. (2007). *Globalization and Militarism: Feminists Make the Link.* Lanham, MD: Rowman and Littlefield.

Epstein, D., Kehily, M.J., & Renold, E. (2012). Culture, Policy and the Un/Marked Child: Fragments of the Sexualisation Debates. *Gender and Education* (Special Issue: Making Sense of the Sexualisation Debates: Schools and Beyond), *24 (3),* 249–254.

Equality and Human Rights Commission. (2010). *Equality Act.* HM Government.

Equal Opportunities Commission. (2001). *Young People and Sex Stereotyping.* (http://www.eoc.org.uk/cseng/research/young_people_and_sex_stererotyping_findings.pdf).

Feiring, C., Deblinger, E., Hoch-Espada, A., & Haworth, T. (2002). Romantic Relationship Aggression and Attitudes in High School Students: the Role of Gender, Grade, and Attachment and Emotional Styles. *Journal of Youth and Adolescence, 31,* 373–385.

Felmlee, D., & Muraco, A. (2009). Gender and Friendship Norms Among Older Adults. *Research on Aging, 31(3),* 318–344.

DOI: 10.1057/9781137365699.0013

Fielding, M., & Bragg, S. (2003). *Students as Researchers: Making a Difference. Consulting Pupils about Teaching and Learning.* Cambridge: Pearson Publishing.

Flood, M. (2001). Men's Collective Anti-Violence Activism and the Struggle for Gender Justice. *Development* (Special Issue: Violence against Women and the Culture of Masculinity), *44,* 42–47.

Flood, M. (2007). Why Violence against Women and Girls Happens, and How to Prevent It. *Redress (August),* 13–19.

Flood, M. (2010). *Where Men Stand: Men's Roles in Ending Violence against Women.* Sydney: White Ribbon Prevention Research Series, No. 2.

Flutter, J. (2006). Engaging Students as Partners in Learning. *Curriculum Briefing, 3,* 3–6.

Fontes, L. A. (1997). Conducting Ethical Cross-Cultural Research on Family Violence. In G. K. Kantor & J. L. Jasinski (Eds), *Out of the Darkness: Contemporary Perspectives on Family Violence* (pp. 296–312). Thousand Oaks, CA: Sage

Fontes, L.A. (2004). Ethics in Violence Against Women Research: The Sensitive, the Dangerous, and the Overlooked. *Ethics and Behaviour, 14(2),* 141–174.

Foshee, V., Reyes, H.L.M., & Ennett, S.T. (2010). Examination of Sex and Race Differences in Longitudinal Predictors of the Initiation of Adolescent Dating Violence Perpetration. *Journal of Aggression, Maltreatment and Trauma, 19 (5),* 492–516.

Foshee, V., Bauman, K. E., Ennett, S. T., Suchindran, C., Benefield, T., & Linder, G. F. (2005). Assessing the Effects of the Dating Violence Prevention Program "Safe Dates" Using Random Coefficient Regression Modeling.*Prevention Science, 6(3),* 245–258.

Foshee, V., Benefield, T.S., Reyes, H.L.M., Ennett, S., Faris, R., Ling-Yin, C., Hussong, A., & Suchindran, C.M. (2013). The Peer Context and the Development of the Perpetration of Adolescent Dating Violence. *Journal of Youth and Adolescence, 42,* 471–486.

Foucault, M. (1975). *Discipline and Punish: the Birth of the Prison.* Paris: Editions Gallimard.

Foucault, M. (1976). *The History of Sexuality (Volume 1: An Introduction).* Paris: Editions Gallimard.

Fox, C.L., Corr, M-L., Gadd, D., & Butler, I. (2013a). Young Teenagers' Experiences of Domestic Abuse. *Journal of Youth Studies.* DOI: http://dx.doi.org/10.1080/13676261.2013.780125.

DOI: 10.1057/9781137365699.0013

Fox C.L., Hale, R., & Gadd, D. (2013b). Domestic Abuse Prevention Education: Listening to the Views of Young People. *Sex Education: Sexuality, Society and Learning,* DOI:10.1080/14681811.2013.816949.

Fox, C.L., Hale, R., & Gadd, D. (2014). Domestic Abuse Preventon Education: Listening to the Views of Young People. *Sex Education; Sexuality, Society and Learning, 14(1),* 28–41. DOI: 10.1080/14681811.2013.816949.

Francis, B. (2008). Teaching Manfully? Exploring Gendered Subjectivities and Power Via Analysis of Men Teachers' Gender Performance. *Gender and Education, 20(2),* 109–122.

Francis, B., & Mills, M. (2012). Schools as Damaging Organisations: Instigating a Dialogue Considering Alternative Models of Schooling. *Culture, Pedagogy & Society, 20(2),* 251–272.

Franzosi, R. (1998). Narrative Analysis – Or Why (and How) Sociologists Should be Interested in Narrative. *Annual Review of Sociology, 24(1),* 517–554.

Fraser, N., & Bartky, S.L. (1992). (Eds.) *Revaluing French Feminism: Critical Essays on Difference, Agency and Culture.* Hypatia, Inc.

Fraser, S., Lewis, V., Ding, S., Kellet, M., & Robinson, C. (2004). *Doing Research with Children and Young People.* London: Sage.

Fredland, N. M., Ricardo, I. B., Campbell, J. C., Sharps, P. W., Kub, J. K., & Yonas, M. (2005). The Meaning of Dating Violence in the Lives of Middle School Adolescents: a Report of a Focus Group Study. *Journal of School Violence, 4,* 95–114.

Furlong, M.J., Felix, E.D., Sharkey, J.D., & Larson, J. (2005). *Preventing School Violence: A Plan for Safe and Engaging Schools.* Bethseda, MD: National Assocation of School Psychologists.

Glaser, B., and A. Strauss. (1967). *The Discovery of Grounded Theory: Strategies for Qualitative Research.* Chicago: Aldine.

Glick, G., & Fiske, S.T. (1996). The Ambivalent Sexism Inventory: Differentiating Hostile and Benevolent Sexism. *Journal of Personality and Social Psychology, 70(3),* 491–512.

Gorman-Smith, D., Henry, D.B. & Tolan, P.H. (2004). Exposure to Community Violence and Violence Perpetration: the Protective Effects of Family Functioning. *Journal of Child Clinical and Adolescent Psychology, 33,* 439–449.

Greytak, E. (2003). Educating for the Prevention of Sexual Abuse: An Investigation of School-Based Programs for High School Students and their Applicability to Urban Schools. *Penn GSE Perspectives on*

DOI: 10.1057/9781137365699.0013

Urban Education, 2 (1). (http://www.urbanedjournal.org/archive/
volume-2-issue-1-spring-2003/educating-prevention-sexual-abuse-
investigation-school-based-pr) (Accessed 10 October 2013).

Gurian, M. (2002). *Boys and Girls Learn Differently!* San Francisco: Jossey
Bass.

Haglund, K., Belknap, R.A., & Garcia, J.T. (2012). Mexican American
Female Adolescents' Perceptions of Relationships and Dating
Violence. *Journal of Nursing Scholarship, 44(3),* 215–222.

Hale, R., Fox, C.L., & Gadd, D. (2012). REaDAPt: Research Report
Evaluation of Three European Schools-Based Domestic Violence
Prevention Education Programmes. University of Keele, EU
Commission (DAPHNE III).

Hamlall, V., & Morrell, R.G. (2012). Conflict, Provocation and Fights
among Boys in a South African High School. *Gender and Education,
24(5),* 483–498.

Hamner, J., & Maynard, M. (1987). *Women, Violence and Social Control.*
Humanities Press International.

Hamner, J., & Saunders, S. (1984). *Well-Founded Fear: a Community
Study of Violence to Women.* Hutchinson, Explorations in Feminism
Collective.

Hazel, N. (1995) Elicitation Techniques with Young People, *Social
Research Update,* Issue 12, Department of Sociology, University
of Surrey (http://sru.soc.surrey.ac.uk/SRU12.html) (Accessed 16
October 2013).

Hearn, J. (1994). The Organization(s) of Violence: Men, Gender
Relations, Organizations, and Violences. *Human Relations, 47 (6),*
731–754.

Hearn, J. (1996). Men's Violence to Known Women: Men's Accounts and
Men's Policy Development. In B. Fawcett, B. Featherstone, J. Hearn &
C. Toft (Eds), *Violence and Gender Relations: Theories and Interventions*
(pp. 99–114). London: Sage.

Hearn, J. (1998). *The Violences of Men How Men Talk About and How
Agencies Respond to Men's Violence to Women.* London: Sage.

Hearn, J. (2004). From Hegemonic Masculinity to the Hegemony of
Men. *Feminist Theory, 5 (1),* 49–72.

Hearn, J. (2007). Theorizing Men's Violences against Known Women:
Or What Sociological Theory Might Learn from Men's Violences to
Known Women. *Research and Development on Social Policies, 2,* 21–38.

DOI: 10.1057/9781137365699.0013

Hearn, J. (2012). a Multi-Faceted Power Analysis of Men's Violence to Known Women: From Hegemonic Masculinity to the Hegemony of Men. *Sociological Review, 60(4),* 589–610.

Hearn, J., & Whitehead, A. (2006). Collateral Damage: Men's Domestic Violence to Women Seen through Men's Relations with Men. *Probation Journal, 53 (1),* 38–56.

Helweg-Larsen K., Sundaram V., Curtis T., & Bøving Larsen H. (2004). The Danish Youth Survey 2002: Asking Young People about Sensitive Issues. *Circumpolar Health Supplement 2,* 147–153.

Helweg-Larsen K., & Boving Larsen, H. (2006). The Prevalence of Unwanted and Unlawful Sexual Experiences Reported by Danish Adolescents: Results from a National Youth Survey in 2002. *Acta Paediatrica, 95(10),* 1270–1276.

Herrman, J. (2013). How Teen Mothers Describe Dating Violence. *Journal of Obstetric Gynaecologic Neonatal Nursing, 42,* 462–470.

Herrman, J.W. & Silverstein, J. (2012). Girls' Perceptions of Violence and Prevention. *Journal of Community Health Nursing, 29 (2),* 75–90.

Hernandez, D., Weinstein, H., & Munoz-Laboy, M. (2012). Youth Perspectives on Instersections of Violence, Gender and Hip-Hop. *Youth & Society, 44(4),* 587–608.

Hester, M., Pearson, C., & Harwin, N. (2000). *Making an Impact: A Reader.* London: Jessica Kingsley.

Hester, M., & Westmarland, N. (2005). *Tackling Domestic Violence: Effective Interventions and Approaches,* London: Home Office.

Holland, J., Ramazanoglu, C., Sharpe, S., & Thomson, R. (1998). *The Male in the Head: Young People, Heterosexuality and Power.* London: The Tufnell Press.

Hollander, J. (2001). Vulnerability and Dangerousness: The Construction of Gender through Conversation about Violence. *Gender & Society, 15(1),* 83–109.

Holstein, J.A., & Gubrium, J.F. (1998). Phenomenology, Ethnomethodology and Interpretive Practice. In N.K. Denzin & Y.S. Lincoln (Eds), *Strategies of Qualitative Inquiry* (pp. 137–157). Thousand Oaks, CA: Sage Publications.

Home Office. (2010). *This Is Abuse.* (http://thisisabuse.direct.gov.uk) (Accessed 16 October 2013).

Home Office. (2011). *Ending Gang and Youth Violence: A Cross-Government Report.* HM Government.

DOI: 10.1057/9781137365699.0013

Home Office (2012). *Cross-Government Definition of Domestic Violence. a Consultation.* Home Office.

Home Office. (2013). *Ending Violence against Women and Girls in the UK.* HM Government, Home Office.

Home Office. (2013). *Addressing Youth Violence and Gangs. Practical Advice for Schools and Colleges.* HM Government, Home Office.

Honkatukia, P., Nyqvist, L., & Pösö, T. (2006). Violence from Within the Reform School. *Youth Violence and Juvenile Justice, 4,* 328–344.

Hoover, H. (2014). 'Your critical tweets about Rhianna's love life are more hurtful than helpful'. (http://www.thegloss.com/2014/02/20/sex-and-dating/rihanna-chris-brown-relationship-tweets/) (Accessed 27 February 2014).

Howard, D.E., Debnam, K.J., & Wang, M.Q. (2013). Ten-Year Trends in Physical Dating Violence Victimization among u.s. Adolescent Females. *Journal of School Health, 83(6),* 389–399.

Humphreys, C., Houghton, C., & Ellis, J. (2008). *Literature Review: Better Outcomes for Children and Young People Affected by Domestic Abuse — Directions for Good Practice.* Edinburgh: The Scottish Government.

Jackson, C. (2002). 'Laddishness' as a Self-worth Protection Strategy. *Gender and Education, 14 (1),* 37–50.

Jackson, C. (2003). Motives for 'Laddishness' at School: Fear of Failure and Fear of the 'Feminine'. *British Educational Research Journal, 29 (4),* 583–598.

Jackson, S.M., Cram, F., & Seymour, F.W. (2000). Violence and Sexual Coercion in High School Students' Dating Relationships. *Journal of Family Violence, 15(1),* 23–36.

Jago, S., & Pearce, J. (2008). *Gathering Evidence of the Sexual Exploitation of Young People. a Scoping Exercise.* Luton: University of Bedfordshire.

James, A., Jenks, C., & Prout, H. (1998). *Theorising Childhood.* Polity Press.

Kaufman, M. (1985). The Construction of Masculinity and the Triad of Men's Violence. In M. Kaufman (Ed.), *Beyond Patriarchy: Essays by Men on Pleasure, Power, and Change* (pp. 1–29). Toronto, ON: Oxford University Press.

Kaufman, M. (2001). Building a Movement of Men to End Violence against Women. *Development, 44(3),* 9–14.

Kehily, M. (2007). A Cultural Perspective. In M.J. Kehily (Ed.), *Understanding Youth: Perspectives, Identities and Practices.* (pp. 11–44). London: Sage and Open University Press.

DOI: 10.1057/9781137365699.0013

Kelly, L. (1988). *Surviving Sexual Violence.* Cambridge, UK: Polity Press.

Kenway, J., & Fitzclarence, L. (1997). Masculinity, Violence and Schooling. Challenging 'Poisonous Pedagogies'. *Gender and Education, 9(1),* 117–134.

Kimmel, M.S., Hearn, J., & Connell, R.W. (Eds) (2005). *Handbook of Studies on Men and Masculinities.* Thousand Oaks and London: Sage Publications.

King, N. M., & Churchill, L. R. (2000). Ethical Principles Guiding Research on Child and Adolescent Subjects. *Journal of Interpersonal Violence, 15,* 710–724.

Kitzinger, J. (1994). The Methodology of Focus Groups: The Importance of Interaction between Research Participants. *Sociology of Health & Illness, 16(1),* 103–121.

Krug, E.G., Brener, N.D., Dahlberg, L.L., Ryan, G.W., & Powell, K.E. (1997). The Impact of An Elementary School-Based Violence Prevention Program on Visits to the School Nurse. *American Journal of Preventive Medicine, 13(6),* 459–463.

Krusemark, S. (2012). The Campus as Stage: A Qualitative Study of the Hypervisibility and Invisibility of African American Female Identity in the Built Campus Environment. *Journal of Research on Women and Gender, 4,* 25–51.

LaCasse, A. and M. Mendelson. (2007). Sexual Coercion among Adolescents: Victims and Perpetrators. *Journal of Interpersonal Violence, 2,* 424–443.

Langhinrichsen-Rohling, J., & Capaldi, D.M. (2012). Clearly We've Only Just Begun: Developing Effective Prevention Programs for Intimate Partner Violence. *Prevention Science, 12,* 410–414.

Lazar, M.M. (2005). Politicising Gender in Discourse: Feminist Critical Discourse Analysis as Perspective and Praxis. In M.M. Lazar (Ed.), *Feminist Critical Discourse Analysis.* London: Palgrave Macmillan.

Li, X., Stanton, B., Pack, R., Harris, C., Cottrell, L., & Burns, J. (2002). Risk and Protective Factors Associated with Gang Involvement among Urban African American Adolescents. *Youth & Society, 34(2),*172–194.

Lohman, B.J., Neppl, T.K., Senia, J.M, & Schofield, T.J. (2013). Understanding Adolescent and Family Influences on Intimate Partner Psychological Violence During Emerging Adulthood and Adulthood. *Journal of Youth and Adolescence, 42,* 500–517.

Lunt, P., & Livingstone, S. (1996). Focus Groups in Communication and Media Research. *Journal of Communication Studies, 42,* 78–87.

DOI: 10.1057/9781137365699.0013

Mac an Ghaill, M. (1994). *The Making of Men: Masculinities, Sexualities and Schooling*. Buckingham, UK: Open University Press.

Mahony , P., & Shaughnessy, J. (2007). Evaluation of WOMANKIND Worldwide's Schools' Pilot Programme. Challenging Violence, Changing Lives. Unpublished.

Maimon, D., & Browning, C.R. (2012). Adolescents' Violent Victimization in the Neighbourhood Situational and Contextual Determinants. *British Journal of Criminology, 52(4),* 808–833.

Mandel, L., & Shakeshaft, C. (2000). Heterosexism in Middle Schools. In N. Lesko (Ed.), *Masculinities at School* (pp. 75–103). Thousand Oaks, CA: Sage.

Martin del Campo, M. A.., Hokoda, A., & Ulloa E. C. (2012). Age and Gender Differences in Teen Relationship Violence. *Journal of Aggression Maltreatment and Trauma, 21,* 351–364.

Martsolf, D. S., Colbert, C., & Draucker, C. B. (2012). Adolescent Dating Violence Prevention and Intervention in a Community Context: Perspectives of Young Adults and Professionals. *The Qualitative Report, 17,* 1–23.

Maschi, T., & Bradley, C. (2008). Exploring the Moderating Influence of Delinquent Peers on the Link between Trauma, Anger and Violence Among Male Youth. Implications for Social Work Practice. *Child and Adolescent Social Work Journal, 25,* 125–138.

Matsueda, R.L., Drakulich, K., Hagan, J., Krivo, L.J., & Peterson, R.D. (2012). Crime, Perceptions of Criminal Injustice and Electoral Politics. In J. Aldrich, & K. McGraw (Eds), *The American National Election Study Book of Ideas* (pp. 323–341). Princeton, NJ: Princeton University Press.

Maxwell, C., Chase, E., Warwick, I., & Aggleton, P. (2010). *Freedom to Achieve: Preventing Violence, Promoting Equality. A Whole School Approach.* London: WOMANKIND Worldwide.

McCarry, M. (2003). *The Connection between Masculinity and Domestic Violence: What Young People Think.* University of Bristol: Unpublished Ph.D. Thesis.

McCarry, M. (2007). Domestic Violence. In M. Flood, J.K. Gardiner, B. Pease, & K.Pringle (Eds), *International Encyclopedia of Men and Masculinities* (pp. 147–151). London and New York: Routledge.

McCarry, M. (2009). Justifications and Contradictions: Understanding Young People's Tolerance of Domestic Abuse. *Men and Masculinities, 11(3),* 325–345.

McCarry, M. (2010). Becoming a 'Proper Man': Young People's Attitudes about Interpersonal Violence and Perceptions of Gender. *Gender and Education, 22(1),* 17–30.

DOI: 10.1057/9781137365699.0013

McCarry, M., Hester, M and Donovan, C. (2008). Researching Same Sex Domestic Violence: Constructing a Survey Methodology . *Sociological Research Online, 13 (1)*.

Measor, L., Tiffin, C. & Miller, K. (2000). *Young People's Views on Sex Education: Education, Attitudes and Behaviour*. London: RoutledgeFalmer.

Messerschmidt, J.W. (2000). *Nine Lives: Adolescent Masculinities, the Body, and Violence*: Westview Press.

Messerschmidt, J.W. (2005). Men, Masculinities and Crime. In M.S. Kimmel, J. Hearn, R.W. Connell (Eds), *Handbook of Studies on Men and Masculinities* (pp. 196–212). London: Sage.

Messerschmidt, J.W. (2012). *Gender, Heterosexuality, and Youth Violence: The Struggle for Recognition*. Lanham, MD: Rowman & Littlefield.

Migliaccio, T.A. (2001). Marginalising the Battered Male. *Journal of Men's Studies, 9*, 205–226.

Miller, W.L., & Crabtree, B.F. (1998). Clinical Research. In N.K. Denzin & Y.S. Lincoln (Eds), *Strategies of Qualitative Inquiry* (pp. 292–314). Thousand Oaks, CA: Sage Publications.

Miller, P. J., Fung, H., & Koven, M. (2007). Narrative Reverberations: How Participation in Narrative Practices Co-Creates Persons and Cultures. In S. Kitayama & D. Cohen (Eds), *Handbook of Cultural Psychology* (pp. 595–614). New York: Guilford.

Mills, M. (2001). *Challenging Violence in Schools: An Issue of Masculinities*. Buckingham: Open University Press.

Mitchell, D., Angelone, D.J., Kohlberger, B., & Hirschman, R. (2009). Effects of Offender Motivation, Victim Gender, and Participant Gender on Perceptions of Rape Victims and Offenders. *Journal of Interpersonal Violence, 24 (9)*, 1564–1578.

Mitra, M., Mouradian, V.E., & McKenna, M. (2013). Dating Violence and Associated Health Risks Among High School Students with Disabilities. *Journal of Maternal and Child Health, 17(6)*, 1088–1094.

Moretti, M.M., Osbuth, I., Odgers, C.L., Reebye, P. (2006). Exposure to Maternal versus Paternal Partner Violence, ptsd, and Aggression in Adolescent Girls and Boys. *Aggressive Behavior, 32*, 385–395.

Morgan, D.H.J. (1987). Masculinity and Violence. In J. Hamner, & M. Maynard (Eds), *Women, Violence and Social Control*. London: Macmillan.

Morgan, D. (1988). *Focus Groups as Qualitative Research*. London: Sage Publications.

DOI: 10.1057/9781137365699.0013

Moules, T. (2009). 'They wouldn't know how it feels': Characteristics of Quality Care from Young People's Perspectives. a Participatory Research Project. *Journal of Child Health Care, 13(4),* 322–332.

Mullaney, J. L. (2007). Telling It Like a Man: Masculinities and Battering Men's Accounts of Their Violence. *Men and Masculinities, 10,* 222–247.

Mullender, A. (2001). Meeting the Needs of Children. In J. Taylor-Browne (Ed.), *What Works in Reducing Domestic Violence?* London: Whiting and Birch Ltd.

Mullender, A., Kelly, L., Hague, G., Malos, E., & Iman, U. (2002). *Children's Perspectives on Domestic Violence.* London: Routledge

Myrttinen, H. (2004). 'Pack your heat and work the streets': Weapons and the Active Construction of Violent Masculinities. *Women and Language, 27(2),* 29–34.

National Health Service. (NHS). (2001). *Teenage Pregnancy: An Update on Key Characteristics of Effective Interventions.* London: Health Development Agency.

NASUWT. (2009). *Preventing and Tackling Prejudice-related Bullying.* Birmingham: NASUWT.

National Working Group (2010). An Interim Report: Special Edition of the What's Going On? Newsletter. *(Autumn).* University of Bedforshire.

Newburn, T., & Stanko, E. (Eds) (1995). *Just Boys Doing Business; Men, Masculinities and Crime.* London: Routledge.

Noonan, R., & Charles, D. (2009). Developing Teen Dating Violence Prevention Strategies: Formative Research With Middle School Youth. *Violence Against Women, 15 (9),* 1087–1105.

NSPCC. (2011). *Child Cruelty in the UK 2011: The facts.* London: NSPCC.

O'Donnell, M., & Sharpe, S. (2000). *Uncertain Masculinities: Youth, Ethnicity and Class in Contemporary Britain.* London: Routledge.

Office for National Statistics. (2012). *Crime in England and Wales, Year ending March 2012.* Statistical Bulletin. (http://www.ons.gov.uk) (Accessed 10 October 2013).

Office for National Statistics. (2013). *Crime in England and Wales, Year ending March 2013.* Statistical Bulletin. (http://www.ons.gov.uk) (Accessed 10 October 2013).

Office of the Children's Commissioner (OCC) (2013). (www.childrenscommissioner.gov.uk) (Accessed 16 October 2013).

Ofsted. (2013). *Not Good Enough Yet: Personal, Social, Health and Economic Education in Schools.* Manchester: Ofsted.

DOI: 10.1057/9781137365699.0013

O'Kane, C. (2008). The Development of Participatory Techniques: Facilitating Children's Views About Decisions Which Affect Them. In P.M. Christensen & A. James (Eds), *Research with Children: Perspectives and Practices* (2nd edn). Oxon and New York: Routledge.

O'Neill, D. (1998). A Post-Structuralist Review of the Theoretical Literature Surrounding Wife Abuse, *Violence Against Women, 4(4),* 457–490.

Orbuch, T. (1997). People's Accounts Count: The Sociology of Accounts. *Annual Review of Sociology, 23,* 455–478.

Osler, A. (2006). Excluded Girls: Interpersonal, Institutional and Structural Violence in Schooling. *Gender and Education, 18 (6),* 571–589.

Osler, A., & Vincent, K. (2003). *Girls and Exclusion: Rethinking the Agenda.* London: Routledge Falmer.

Ozer, E. J. (2006). Contextual Effects in School-Based Violence Prevention Programs: a Conceptual Framework and Empirical Review. *Journal of Primary Prevention, 27(3),* 315–340.

Paechter, C.F. (2010). Tomboys and Girly-Girls: Embodied Femininities in Primary Schools. *Discourse 31(2),* 221–235.

Palmetto, N., Davidson, L.L., Breitbart, V., & Rickert, V.I. (2013). Predictors of Physical Intimate Partner Violence in the Lives of Young Women: Victimization, Perpetration, and Bidirectional Violence. *Violence and Victims, 20(1),* 103–121.

Pearce, J. and Pitts, J. (2011) *Youth Gangs, Sexual Violence and Sexual Exploitation: A Scoping Exercise for The Office of the Children's Commissioner for England* (http://www.beds.ac.uk/intcent/ publications). Accessed 22 April 2014.

Polkinghorne, D.E. (2007). Validity Issues in Narrative Research. *Qualitative Inquiry, 13(4),* 471–486.

Pösö, T., Honkatukia, P., & Nyqvist, L. (2008). Focus Groups and the Study of Violence. *Qualitative Research, 8,* 73–89.

Próspero, M. (2006a). Middle School Students' Aggressive Reactions to Dating Situations. *Journal of School Violence 5(4),*65–77.

Próspero, m. (2006b). The Role of Perceptions in Dating Violence among Young Adolescents. *Journal of Interpersonal Violence, 21(4),* 470–484.

Read, B. (2011). Britney, Beyonce and Me – Primary School Girls' Role Models and Constructions of the 'Popular' Girl. *Gender and Education, 23(1),* 1–13.

DOI: 10.1057/9781137365699.0013

Reay, D. (2001). 'Spice Girls', 'Nice Girls', 'Girlies', and 'Tomboys': Gender Discourses, Girls' Cultures and Femininities in the Primary Classroom. *Gender and Education, 13(2),* 153–166.

Renold, E. (2006). Gendered Classroom Experiences. In C. Skelton, B. Francis & L. Smulyan (Eds), *The SAGE Handbook of Gender and Education* (pp. 439–452). London: Sage Publications.

Renold, E., & Barter, C. (2003). 'Hi, i'm Ramon and i Run This Place': Challenging the Normalisation of Peer Violence in Children's Homes. In E. Stanko (Ed.) *The Meaning of Violence* (pp. 90–111). London: Routledge.

Renold, E., & Ringrose, J. (2011). Schizoid Subjectivities: Re-Theorising Teen-Girls' Sexual Cultures in An Era of Sexualisation. *Journal of Sociology, special issue – 'Youth identities, Cultures and Transitions'. 47(4),* 389–409.

Richards, A., Rivers, I., & Ackhurts, J. (2008). a Positive Psychology Approach to Tackling Bullying in Secondary Schools. a Comparative Evaluation. *Educational and Child Psychology,* 25(2), 72–81.

Rights of Women (2010) *Measuring Up?* uk *Compliance with International Commitments on Violence against Women in England and Wales.* London: ROW.

Rose, R., & Shevlin, M. (2004). Encouraging Voices: Listening to Young People Who Have Been Marginalised, *Support for Learning 19 (4),* 155–161.

Sauntson, H. (2012). *Approaches to Gender and Spoken Classroom Discourse.* Basingstoke: Palgrave Macmillan.

Schutz, A. (1970). *On Phenomenology and Social Relations.* Evanstone, IL: Northwestern University Press.

Sears, H.A., Byers, S.E., Whelan, J.J., & Saint-Pierre, M. (2006). 'If it hurts, then it's not a joke'. Adolescents' Ideas about Girls' and Boys' Use and Experience of Abusive Behaviour in Dating Relationships. *Journal of Interpersonal Violence, 21(9),* 1191–1207.

Sex Education Forum. (2013). *Sex Education Forum Response to Welsh Government Consultation on Legislation to End Violence against Women and Domestic Abuse.* (retrieved from http://www.sexeducationforum. org.uk/media/12752/sef__welsh_government_proposals_on_ evawg_-_feb_2013.pdf).

Shortt, J.W., Capaldi, D.M., Kim, H.K., & Tiberio, S.S. (2013). The Interplay between Interpersonal Stress and Psychological Intimate Partner Violence Over Time for Young At-Risk Couples *Journal of Youth and Adolescence, 42,* 619–632.

DOI: 10.1057/9781137365699.0013

Simonson, K., & Subich, L. (1999). Rape Perceptions as a Function of Gender-Role Traditionality and Victim-Perpetrator Association. *Sex Roles, 40,* 617–634.

Skelton, C. (2006). Boys and Girls in the Elementary School. In C. Skelton, B. Francis, & L. Smulyan (Eds), *The SAGE Handbook of Gender and Education* (pp.139–151). London: Sage Publications.

Skelton, C., Francis, B., Carrington, B., Hutchings, M., Read, B., & Hall, I. (2009). Primary Teachers' Perceptions of Gender and Its Significance for Teaching and Managing Pupils. *British Educational Research Journal, 35(2),* 187–204.

Skelton, C., Francis, B., & Read, B. (2010). 'Brains before Beauty?' High Achieving Girls, School and Gender Identities. *Educational Studies, 36(2),* 185–194.

Smith, P. K., Morita, J., Junger-Tas, D., Olweus, D., Catalano, R., & Slee, P. T. (Eds) (1999). *The Nature of School Bullying: a Cross-National Perspective.* London: Routledge.

Smith A., Winokur K., & Palenski J. (2005). What Is Dating Violence? An Exploratory Study of Hispanic Adolescent Definitions. *Journal of Ethnicity in Criminal Justice, 3,* 1–20.

Sommer, M., Likindikoki, S., & Kaaya, S. (2013). Boys' and Young Men's Perspectives on Violence In Northern Tanzania. *Culture, Health & Sexuality, 15(6),* 695–709.

Spencer, G., Maxwell, C., & Aggleton, P. (2008). What Does 'Empowerment' Mean in School-Based Sex and Relationships Education? *Sex Education, 8,* 345–356.

Stader, D.L. (2011). Dating Violence. *The Clearing House: A Journal of Educational Strategies, Issues and Ideas, 84,* 139–143.

Stanko, E. (1990). *Everyday Violence: How Women and Men Experience Physical and Sexual Danger.* London: Pandora Press.

Stanko, E. (2002). *The Meanings of Violence.* London: Routledge.

Stanley, N., Ellis, J., & Bell, J. (2011). Delivering Preventative Programmes in Schools: Identifying Gender Issues. In C. Barter & D. Berridge (Eds), *Children Behaving Badly? Peer Violence Between Children and Young People* (pp. 217–230). Chichester: Wiley-Blackwell.

Stephenson, J.M., Strange, V., Forrest, S., Oakley, A., Copas, A., Allen, E., Babiker, A., Black, S., Ali, M., Monteiro, H., Johnson, A.M., & RIPPLE study team. (2004). Pupil-Led Sex Education in England (ripple Study): Cluster-Randomised Intervention Trial. *Lancet, 364(9431),* 338–346.

DOI: 10.1057/9781137365699.0013

Stoudt, B.G. (2006). "You're Either In or You're Out": School Violence, Peer Discipline and the (Re)production of Hegemonic Masculinity. *Men and Masculinities, 8,* 273–287.

Sullivan, T.N., Erwin, E.H., Helms, S.W., Masho, S.W., & Farrell, A.D. (2010). Problematic Situations Associated with Dating Experiences and Relationships among Urban African American Adolescents: A Qualitative Study. *Journal of Primary Prevention, 31(5),* 365–378.

Sullivan, T.N., Helms, S.W., Bettencourt, A.F., Sutherland, K., Lotze, G.M., Mays, S., Wright, S., & Farrell, A.D. (2012). A Qualitative Study of Individual and Peer Factors Related to Effective Nonviolent versus Aggressive Responses to Problem Situations among Adolescents with High Incidence Disabilities. *Behavioral Disorders 37(3),* 163–178.

Sundaram V., Laursen B., Helweg-Larsen K. (2008). Is Sexual Victimisation Gender-Specific? the Prevalence of Forced Sexual Activity Among Men and Women in Denmark, and Self-Reported Well-Being Among Survivors. *Journal of Interpersonal Violence, 23 (10),* 1414–1440.

Sundaram, V. (2010). Gender and Education. In J. Arthur & I. Davies (Eds), *The Routledge Textbook on Education Studies* (pp. 50–60). London: Routledge.

Taylor, T.J., Freng, A., Esbensen, F-A., Peterson, D. (2008). Youth Gang Membership and Serious Violent Victimization: The Importance of Lifestyles and Routine Activities. *Journal of Interpersonal Violence, 23(10),* 1441–1464.

Temple, J. R., Le, V.D., Muir, A., Goforth, L., McElhany, A.L. (2013). The Need for School-Based Teen Dating Violence Prevention. *Journal of Applied Research on Children: Informing Policy for Children at Risk, 4(1),* 1–11.

Thornton, T.N., Craft, C.A., Dahlberg, L.L., Lynch, B.S., & Baer, K. (2000). *Best Practices of Youth Violence Prevention: A Community Source Handbook.* National Centre for Injury Prevention and Control. Atlanta, GA: Centres for Disease Control and Prevention.

Tjaden, P., & Thoennes, N. (2000). *Extent, Nature, and Consequences of Intimate Partner Violence.* Washington, DC: US Department of Justice, Office of Justice Programs, National Institute of Justice.

Totten, M. (2003). Girlfriend Abuse as a Form of Masculinity Construction amongst Violent, Marginal Male Youth. *Men and Masculinities, 6(1),* 70–92.

Turner, H.A., Shattuck, A., Hamby, S., & Finkelhor, D. (2013). Community Disorder, Victimization Exposure, and Mental Health in

DOI: 10.1057/9781137365699.0013

a National Sample of Youth. *Journal of Health and Social Behavior, 54* (2), 257–274.

Tutty, L., Bradshaw, K., Thurston, W.E., Barlow, A., Marshall, P., Tunstall, L. et al. (2005). *School-Based Violence Prevention Programs:* a *Resource Manual. Preventing Violence against Children and Youth* (2005 revision). University of Manitoba, RESOLVE Alberta.

Ulloa, E.C., Jaycox, S.K., Skinner, L.H., & Orsburn, M.M. (2008). Attitudes about Violence and Dating Among Latina/o Boys and Girls. *Journal of Ethnic and Cultural Diversity in Social Work, 17(2),* 157–176.

United Nations (1989). United Nations Convention on the Rights of the Child. (http://www.unicef.org/crc/) (Accessed 10 October 2013).

United States Department of Health and Human Services (2001). (http://www.surgeongeneral.gov/news/2001/01/youth-violence.html) (Accessed 18 October 2013).

Vagi, K.J., Rothman, E.F., Latzman, N.E., Tharp, A.T., Hall, D.M., & Breiding, M.J. (2013). Beyond Correlates: A Review of Risk and Protective Factors for Adolescent Dating Violence Perpetration, *Journal of Youth and Adolescence 42,* 633–649.

Varnava, G. (2009). *Checkpoints for Schools: towards a Non-Violent Society. Improving Behaviour for Better Learning.* London, National Society for the Prevention of Cruelty to Children.

Van de Veur, D., Vrethem, K., Titley, G., & Tóth, G. (2007). *Gender Matters:* a *Manual on Addressing Violence Affecting Young People.* Budapest: Directorate of Youth and Sport, Council of Europe.

Viki, G.T., Abrams, D., & Masser, B. (2004). Evaluating Stranger and Acquaintance Rape: The Role of Benevolent Sexism in Perpetrator Blame and Recommended Sentence Length. *Law and Human Behaviour, 28,* 295–303.

Vitacco, M.J., Neumann, C.S., & Caldwell, M.F. (2010). Predicting Antisocial Behavior in High-Risk Male Adolescents: Contributions of Psychopathy and Instrumental Violence. *Criminal Justice and Behavior, 37,* 833–846.

Walker, S., Sanci, L., & Temple-Smith, M. (2011). Sexting and Young People: Experts' Views. *Youth Studies Australia, 30(4),* 8–16.

Walsh, C.A., Macmillan, H.L., Trocme, N., Jamieson, E., & Boyle, M.H. (2008). Measurement of Victimisation in Adolescence: Development and Validation of Childhood Experiences of Violence Questionnaire. *Child Abuse & Neglect, 32(11),* 1037–1057.

DOI: 10.1057/9781137365699.0013

Walton, M.D., Harris, A.R., & Davidson, A.J. (2009). "It Makes Me a Man from the Beating I Took": Gender and Aggression in Children's Narratives about Conflict. *Sex Roles, 61,* 383–398.

Wang, X., Petula, S., & Ying H. (2007). "My Sassy Girl": A Qualitative Study of Women's Aggression in Dating Relationships in Beijing. *Journal of Interpersonal Violence, 22(5),* 623–638.

Watson, S. (2007). Boys, Masculinity and School Violence: Reaping What We Sow. *Gender and Education, 16(6),* 729–737.

Weedon, C. (1987). *Feminist Practice and Poststructuralist Theory.* Oxofrd: Blackwell.

Wekerle, C., & Tanaka, M. (2010). Adolescent Dating Violence Research and Violence Prevention: An Opportunity to Support Health Outcomes. *Journal of Aggression, Maltreatment and Trauma, 19(6),* 681–698.

Welsh Assembly Government. (2010). *The Right to Be Safe.* (retrieved from http://wales.gov.uk/docs/dsjlg/publications/commsafety/100325 besafefinalenv1.pdf), Crown Copyright.

Whitaker, D. J., Morrison, S., Lindquist, C., Hawkins, S. R., O'Neil, J. A., Neiis, A.M., Matthew, A., & Reese, L. (2006). a Critical Review of Interventions for the Primary Prevention of Perpetration of Partner Violence. *Aggression and Violent Behavior, 11,* 151–166.

White, R., & Cuneen, C. (2006). Social Class, Youth Crime and Justice. In B. Goldson & J. Muncie (Eds). *Youth Crime and Justice* (pp. 17–29). London: Sage Publications.

White Ribbon Campaign (2013). http://www.whiteribboncampaign. co.uk/ (Accessed 16 October 2013).

Willis, P. (1977). *Learning to Labour: How Working Class Kids Get Working Class Jobs.* Colombia University Press.

Wilson, M., & Daly, M. (1985). Competitiveness, Risk Taking, and Violence: the Young Male Syndrome. *Ethology and Sociobiology, 6,* 59–73.

Wodak, R. (2008). Controversial Issues in Feminist Critical Discourse Analysis. In K. Harrington, L. Litosseliti, H. Sauntson, & J. Sunderland (Eds), *Gender and Language* (pp. 193–210). Basingstoke: Palgrave Macmillan.

Wolfe, D. A., Crooks, C., Jaffe, P., Chiodo, D., Hughes, R., Ellis, W., Stitt, L., & Donner, A. (2009). a School-Based Program to Prevent Adolescent Dating Violence: a Cluster Randomized Trial. *Archives of Pediatric Adolescent Medicine, 163(8),* 692–699.

DOI: 10.1057/9781137365699.0013

Wood, E. (2003). The Power of Pupil Perspectives in Evidence-based Practice: The Case of Gender and Underachievement. *Research Papers in Education* [on-line], *18(4)*, 365–383.

Wood, S., Bellis, M.A., & Watts, C. (2010). *Intimate Partner Violence:* a *Review of Evidence for Prevention.* Centre for Public Health, Liverpool John Moores University.

Wood, M., Barter, C., & Berridge, D. (2011). *Standing on My Own Two Feet: Disadvantaged Teenagers, Intimate Partner Violence and Coercive Control.* London: NSPCC.

Worden, A.P., & Carlson, B.E. (2005). 'Attitudes and Beliefs about Domestic Violence: Results of a Public Opinion Survey' (II. Beliefs about Causes)'. *Journal of Interpersonal Violence,* 20, 1219–1243.

World Health Organisation (2002). *World Report on Violence and Health.* Geneva: World Health Organisation.

World Health Organisation (2010). *Violence Prevention: The Evidence (Changing Cultural and Social Norms That Support Violence).* Liverpool John Moores University, World Health Organisation.

Yamawaki, N. (2007). Rape Perception and the Function of Ambivalent Sexism and Gender-Role Traditionality. *Journal of Interpersonal Violence, 22(4),* 406–423.

Yick, A.G. (2000). Domestic Violence Beliefs and Attitudes in the Chinese American Community. *Journal of Social Service Research 27(1),* 29–51.

Zweig, J, M., Dank, M., Yahner, J., & Lachman, P. (2013). The Rate of Cyber Dating Abuse among Teens and How It Relates to Other Forms of Teen Dating Violence. *Journal of Youth and Adolescence,* 42 (7), 1063–1077.

DOI: 10.1057/9781137365699.0013

Index

adolescents, *see* young people
Annual School Census (ASC)
    database, 29
Asians, 50–1

boys, violence by/between, 3, 46
British Crime Survey, 48
British Educational Research
    Association (BERA), 13–14
bullying, 4

celebrity couples, domestic
    violence among, 2
child health, 2
child-led violence prevention,
    13–15
child maltreatment, 4
child protections/safeguarding,
    20, 24, 86–7
collective violence, 6, 17
Criminal Justice Act, 48
critical masculinities, 6
critical youth studies, 5, 6

dating violence, 12, 45
discourse, 6, 9, 19, 42, 52, 56,
    58, 60, 68, 71–2, 74, 76,
    78–81, 90, 96, 98, 100–1
domestic violence, 2, 4, 19, 45,
    46, 51, 66, 68, 78–9, 81

elder abuse, 4
ethical considerations, 38–40
Every Child Matters, 7

femininity, 24, 56, 73, 102
feminist, 2, 23, 75, 88
    post-structuralism, 6
    scholarship, 18, 41, 60
focus groups, 31–8

gang violence, 3
gender
    concept of, 18–19
    discourses, 6
    expectations, 3, 7, 9, 18,
        20–4, 26, 28, 41, 43, 57, 61,
        63, 65, 67–74, 79–84, 95,
        99, 101–3
    identity, 6
    inequality, 41
    masculinity and, 18
    norms, 3, 9, 18, 20, 22, 24, 41,
        62–6, 68–71, 74–6, 82–4,
        95, 101–2
    role of, in schools, 8–10
    schools and, 8–10, 87–8,
        89–103
    violence and, 2–3, 16–24,
        27–8, 41, 46–7
    in youth narratives of
        violence, 64–84
girls
    violence against, 2, 3, 12,
        19–20, 21
    violence by/between, 46, 71–2

hegemonic masculinity, 18–19, 65
human nature, 77–8

DOI: 10.1057/9781137365699.0014